"Of course Melissa takes a unique perspective in *The New Global Manager*. She seamlessly bridges leadership qualities like empathy and global mindset with hard business tactics that encourage critical thinking. I would highly recommend this book to any leader who would like to see more innovation and sustainable success in their team."

David Hutchison,
SVP Global Business Development at SAP

"*The New Global Manager* breaks down the dynamics of managing into easily digestible pieces. Melissa helps to sophisticate managers, new and experienced, by sharing models and strategies that directly deal with the complex nature of global business today. I would highly recommend you read her book if you would like to be a better manager."

Pierre-Pascal Urbon,
CEO SMA Solar Technology AG

"With a fresh new approach, Melissa Lamson inspires and guides managers to successfully lead diverse, global teams in a 21st century complex global environment. Her very wise and practical global management book is a much needed direct and to the point guide. Today's managers will benefit from understanding how to lead without authority with knowledge about culture, personality and new ways of managing."

Karen S. Walch, PhD,
Author, *Quantum Negotiation: The Art of Getting What You Need*

"Melissa advances our traditional understanding of management by ensuring today's managers understand that all dimensions of diversity impact successful interaction. In *The New Global Manager*, Melissa presents frameworks for managing globally we haven't seen before."

Lori Allen,

Senior Director Human Resources, LinkedIn

"In today's global economy, every successful manager must master the art of managing a diverse team. Melissa Lamson adeptly dissects and clarifies the complexities facing today's leaders. More importantly, she provides the tools, such as OAR™ - a communication model based on observing, asking and reacting, required to overcome the challenges of leading and managing in a multicultural workplace."

Mary-Sara Jones,

Industry Lead, Health & Human Services, IBM

THE NEW GLOBAL MANAGER

THE NEW GLOBAL MANAGER

Learning to Manage Well
in a Complex Business Environment

MELISSA LAMSON

Foreword by Dr. Denis Leclerc
Professor at Thunderbird School of Global Management

Thank You, Interviewees
Lori Allen
Bernd Aundrup
Rami Branitzky
Ralf Drews
Anja Elfner
Christoph Hütton
Jean-Philippe Mula
Jamie O'Sullivan
Phyllis Stewart Pires
Steffen Protsch
Kevin Romito
Marc Underwood
Margit Wintterle
Andy Yasutake
Thank You, Friends and Family
Larry Anderson
Wally Bock
Amy Brown
Shaw Dunton
Max Lamson
Nadra Newash
Jeremy Stover

TABLE OF CONTENTS

PROFESSOR DENIS LECLERC

I was honored to have this fascinating conversation about global leadership with Dr. Denis Leclerc, Professor at Thunderbird School of Global Management. He is a true expert in the field of global management and his signature courses are Cross Cultural Communication and Global Negotiations. Additionally, Dr. Leclerc leads workshops and consults with managers and leaders in organizations globally.

MELISSA: *In your experience and expert opinion, Denis, how has the concept of "managing globally" evolved?*

DENIS: In the last 30 years one of the biggest changes is that people used to be trained to go to another country. Today, most global managers are now managing global teams from their home country, and even from their home office. Learning a foreign language has not been perceived as important and as companies grow from local, national, to now international and global, there is a new sense of knowledge transfer. An international organization will usually send its best managers to a foreign country. A global company has to send the best person regardless of the country of birth or language. That requires a very different need from the HR department. It is not only that the individual needs to learn skills relative to the nation they are sent to, they also have to understand how the knowledge transfer is decentralized.

Most global HR programs are still set up from the headquarters without a true discovery of the needs of its different entities or locations. Some of the biggest challenges that have already been seen are globalization, trade liberalization, and digitalization, but also global competition. There is a severe war for the best talent, and how "the best" is defined is a totally different animal in today's global market.

For example, we say here in the US, that leaders have to be transparent, or they have to coach and empower their employees. That works here, but if you go to other countries that are extremely hierarchical, there is no way you're going to tell a CEO or a VP that they need to be transparent. Information is power and its important -almost critical- for leaders to have the full picture and decide if and what information gets disseminated so as not to disrupt the status quo.

So, this is the evolution, when programs are offered around the world, one has to focus on what it means to be a successful global leader. Companies do not want to talk about communication, even though at the core, that is their biggest problem. But it is easier to talk about the cognitive process of leadership instead of learning new behaviors. However, the fact that your German engineers can't talk to your Brazilian engineers is a communication issue.

MELISSA: *So, understanding communication is key to being a successful global manager. But what else is important about managing globally today?*

DENIS: For most organizations global diversity is not a new HR trend. However, their business challenge is still creating an environment of inclusion with their global workforce. Most managers have to learn not only to communicate with each other but with people from different cultures (e.g. language, non-verbal behavior, how others are motivated, delivering feedback). There is a need to translate a company strategy into a myriad of contexts and cultures. This requires a much higher level of mindset, a true global mindset. Leaders of the future will have to be transcultural.

One can be taught about the way cultures view a particular dimension like time management. That's easy. The challenge is what one does with that information. How does one react? How does one feel? Do they get mad when people don't show up on time? That's what a leader should ask themselves.

A lot of the researchers in Europe, who talk about cross-cultural communication, instead use the word "transcultural", which are people who are able to work and lead across cultures. And that is a much more interesting concept than that of "emotional intelligence" which is what we use in the US more often today. It's an important idea and it has a lot of research behind it, too, but people forget there are also a lot of dark sides to emotional intelligence. That's it's potentially a whole field of manipulation. People who are very good at manipulation have very high level of emotional intelligence.

MELISSA: *That's an important point. Is there a leader you believe embodies the term "transcultural"?*

DENIS: The European definition of a "transcultural leader" is all encompassing, it's more than "international" and more fitting for managing globally. For example, Carlos Ghosn, CEO of Renault, is truly a transcultural leader. He's Brazilian, Lebanese and French -but he's just somebody who's trying to get something done- in a global context.

MELISSA: *So Denis, what do you think global management will look like in the future?*

DENIS: Successful organizations of the future are the ones that will not only manage digitalization but actually to be able to truly manage human capabilities. Technology will become critical but only in the service of human capacities. Global organizations have already moved from local teams or regional teams to nodes of knowledge sharing through products, customer trends and market growth. Leaders of the future have to move from a "world of problems" to a "world of dilemmas" That is, making sense of decision-making or interactions, engagement with uncertainty, and patience.

In global organizations, the changes coming with digitization are rapid and companies are bonding to this technology. It's all about online now. And yes, one can do online, but it doesn't have the depth. We have increased the width because it's possible to chat with 10,000 people at the same time. But the depth of the engagement is very shallow. There are advantages and disadvantages to this and a true global leader needs to know the difference. Especially when it comes to the future, human interaction will be the priority.

MELISSA: *That's right. There's a whole different filter system -or less of a filter system- than when it's in-person, which I think is necessary for true global management.*

DENIS: Yes, organizations have bought into technology solving all our problems. And it helps us much of the time, but also, we don't want to forget that if we are really trying to up-skill global leaders, they are human beings, and you need to have that human interaction. You cannot manage in a matrix without having these human interactions.

MELISSA: *That's a good point, there's so much talk today about leading without authority—we have team leads, matrix teams, and dispersed teams, and all of this, needs leadership from individuals within the team.*

But without an actual title or true authority, how is this going to work globally?

DENIS: The biggest change or the biggest challenge that organizations are not ready for, is working in that matrix. That's something they don't train people, and they don't realize the added complexity of working like that.

With prof Youngdhal, a colleague of mine we have been interviewing in the last 10 years over 2,500 executives, managers, leaders, and people working in 20 different organizations. Still in 2018, the results show that 50 percent of their challenges are with managing teams. And they meant "managing teams" in terms of the diversity, the complexity of those teams, motivations, topics that have been the core of leadership for the last 30 years. To me technology has not help, it has just compounded our interactions.

One of the other surprising aspects of this research relates to the question: 40% indicated that they have challenges influencing upward, not to their own teams, but to people higher up in the organization. The last surprising answer is that 10% talked about their challenges at managing themselves, that is, being under extreme stress. In academia it is called self-leadership.

It's a mix between leadership and behavioral change. The idea is that the executive shouldn't be exhausted. And it's not only the physical exhaustion it's the mental exhaustion. They make mistakes because their brain does not have energy. We talk about global leaders, and what happens if we're not giving them the time to decompress. That is where we have people making some bad decisions and sending inappropriate emails.

And that's why organizations of the future are actually the ones who understand that human interaction is crucial. They understand they have to spend the money on that human interaction, whether it's allowing global teams to travel and meet face-to-face sometimes, or they hire consultants to teach in-person workshops on management skills. Anything that has to do with the soft skills, at some point, has to be recognized, taught and refined. There really is no other way.

MELISSA: *Agreed. Thank you, Denis.*

THE NEW GLOBAL BUSINESS ENVIRONMENT

This time, it really *is* different.

That hit me one day while I was preparing to lead a workshop for one of my large global clients. There were twenty new managers in my class, and they all worked in the US. Most of them grew up here, but only two were classically "White Anglo-Saxon" or what has been traditionally thought of as the "typical American."

When I started my consulting business twenty-plus years ago, white men would have made up almost the whole class. Back then, diversity and inclusion initiatives were just getting off the ground. Back then, you could spend an entire career in a US corporation doing business in our huge domestic market. Back then, your colleagues and your customers would be mostly people like you, if you were a white American male who grew up in the US.

Today, almost every workforce is diverse. There are people from all backgrounds, countries and cultures. We work remotely, virtually and globally. There are more women, different age groups, people with diverse abilities, preferences, religions and languages. And all of this diversity drives a plethora of different approaches in today's business world. It's exciting and complex at the same time.

"Culture" is the name we give to the norms, perceptions, and values that drive our behavior and that we use to evaluate the behavior of other people. When everyone has the same norms, perceptions, and values, interacting with others and doing business is pretty straightforward and easy.

Things get trickier when people whose norms, perceptions, and values are different become your customers, colleagues, or bosses. That makes things harder because of something rooted in human nature.

You make your choices based on your culture, but people evaluate your actions based on their culture. Americans, for example, love e-mail. We like that it's a quick, simple, and effective way to share information. We don't see e-mail as "personal" at all, and that puts us at odds with almost every other culture in the world.

Our "businesslike" e-mail style is often seen by people from other cultures as impolite at best and uncaring at worst. You can't develop good business relationships that way. You have to learn to adapt your style so you're effective with people from a different culture. You have to work with them to make sure the message that gets sent is the same as the message that gets heard.

That's not too bad if you're aware of the potential problem and if you can interact with one culture at a time. That's how things were when I started my consulting practice.

Most of my work in those days was helping business people from one culture learn about how to do business with people from another culture. I helped Americans who wanted to do business with people from India learn what to expect and how to act (and not act). I helped Germans who wanted to do business in the United States understand American actions that made no sense to them.

The good news was that you could learn your way around doing business with people from another culture fairly easily. If you were being transferred to the Paris office, or if you were assigned the new account with that Japanese customer, you could get help figuring things out.

There were books and videos and consultants like me that could help you. You could talk with other managers who had already faced the same challenge. Those books are still around. They'll still help if you have to adjust to only one culture that's different from your own. The challenge is that you may have to understand many cultures at once, like Karen, who was in my class recently.

When the training was over, Karen returned to Austin, Texas. Her team includes people who grew up in several different cultures. In addition to the team of people in Austin, Karen is also responsible for virtual teams that include people in Dublin, India, and Puerto Rico.

Karen's cultural challenge isn't learning to understand a single different culture. She has to relate to people from many cultures and countries on a daily basis. That's not unique today.

If you're an American manager today, you probably work in the kind of environment we used to call "multicultural." Currently, I call it simply, "global." There are three big reasons why today's managers are working in a New Global Environment. Let's start with the most obvious: more US companies are doing business globally than ever before.

MORE US COMPANIES
ARE DOING BUSINESS GLOBALLY

More and more American companies are doing business globally. A recent *US News and World Report* article said:

> "The data show that for most big US firms, foreign sales are a significant portion of total revenues, while firms with little or no foreign revenue are the exception."

A full 40 percent of profit for S&P 500 firms is generated outside the United States. The number is even bigger for some large companies. Procter & Gamble's headquarters are in Cincinnati, but they do business in 180 countries. And almost two-thirds of P&G revenue comes from operations outside the US.

In the last twenty years, the increase in global business by US companies had led to a dramatic increase in Americans working for global corporations. According to the Business Roundtable, global American companies employ 41 million people in the United States—almost three times the number in 1992.

Increasing global activity by American companies is only one force driving the New Global Environment. The US has also experienced a major change in the makeup of our population in the last twenty years.

US DEMOGRAPHICS HAVE CHANGED DRAMATICALLY

The Kauffman Foundation says that, between 2006 and 2012, more than 40 percent of tech start-ups had at least one founder who was born outside the US. In fact, the research firm EthniFacts say that their analysis reveals that the US has become a "multicultural majority nation." They even identified the date when that happened: August 22, 2014. Here's how they came up with that finding.

> "This new 2014 tipping point was calculated by Ethni-Facts using the Interethnic Proximity Index (IPI), a proprietary algorithm that takes into account multiracial

populations, intermarried couples, mixed households, and residence location among other factors to provide a truer indicator of multicultural influence in American society and New Mainstream consumer markets."

You may not agree with the specifics of EthniFacts' findings or the specific date when American society reached a tipping point. But if you look around, you'll probably agree that they got the important parts right. So, you may be asking, "How did this happen?"

To answer that question, you have to go all the way back to 1965, when the US changed its immigration policy. Before 1965, immigrants from England, Ireland, and Germany were entitled to a quota of 70 percent of available visas. The Immigration and Nationality Act of 1965 eliminated the quota system.

Under the old system, immigrants from Asian countries accounted for only 3 percent of visas. Immigrants from Latin America and the Caribbean accounted for 9 percent. Compare that to 2013. That year, more than half of all immigrants came from Latin America and the Caribbean, and slightly more than a quarter came from Asia.

Immigrants brought their children to the US. They had children after they arrived. Those children grew up in the United States, shaped by their parents' culture and the world around them. Most maintained dual languages and cultures, which is an enormous business advantage today!

Karen is a living example of the demographic changes that have transformed America. Her parents were born and raised in China. They brought her here as a baby. She grew up in a mixed community on the West Coast, where she was often the interpreter for her parents. She went to the local public schools and a Quaker college.

Changes in US demographics are a second major force creating the New Global Environment. You'll find that more and more of the Americans you interact with have some roots in a culture that's different from your own. And it will be increasingly hard to know just what those roots are.

We often make assumptions about people based on first impressions. Recently I was doing some training for one of my clients, and there was a white American woman in the room. I made some assumptions about her knowledge of other cultures and her international business experience, based on our initial interaction.

Wow—was I surprised! It turned out she had lived outside the United States for some time and, in fact, spoke fluent Japanese. I should have known better. I should have observed more and asked more questions before I assumed something based on first impressions alone.

Let's return to Karen. She's the product of several cultural influences. At face value, you can't see the influence of the diverse neighborhood where she grew up or some of the values she picked up in college. One of the challenges of the New Global Environment is that you won't always be able to identify any single culture that influences the behavior of the people you work with.

You'll have to stay alert and agile to adjust your behavior to the people and situations you come in contact with. And it's increasingly likely that you will work for someone who was formed by a mix of diverse experiences.

MORE AMERICAN MANAGERS WORK FOR COMPANIES HEADQUARTERED OUTSIDE THE US

There are more foreign-owned companies in the US than ever before. Companies based outside the US employ 5 percent of the American workforce, according to the Brookings Institution. Those workers are scattered across the United States, in cities like Milwaukee, Indianapolis, and Kansas City.

Kansas City is a good example of how many communities have changed. It's right in the middle of the US, the area lots of people call "The Heartland." But the number of people employed by non-US corporations in Kansas City more than doubled between 1991 and 2011. That gives managers like Sam a special challenge.

Sam has all the same challenges that Karen has. Her American team members come from many diverse cultures and, of course, have different personalities. Like Karen, she is responsible for virtual project teams that include team members who grew up, live, and work outside the US.

Sam also has an additional challenge.

The senior management of Sam's company and Sam's boss come from South Korea. Sam is steeped in the American way of doing things. She was born, raised, and went to college in Missouri, and many of her boss's expectations don't make sense to her.

Every week, for example, Sam's boss sends her a detailed work plan. Sam would prefer to have a meeting with her boss every week about what needs to be done. She'd like to develop the work plan with her boss, like her friends at American companies do. She's tried to talk to her boss about this, but it hasn't gone well. She's learning as she goes, often the hard way.

IT DOESN'T HAVE TO BE HARD

The New Global Environment is all around us. Immigration and globalization trends will not reverse any time soon. They will drive the environment you work in every day. Advances in technology further stir the pot, making it more likely that you will have frequent contact with people with diverse norms, perceptions, and values. It's exciting and, at the same time, challenging.

You have two choices. You can do what Sam is doing—learning by trial and error. Or you can master the art of the New Global Manager.

CHAPTER 1

BECOMING A NEW GLOBAL MANAGER

Congratulations. You're a manager, and you have one of the most important jobs in business. You're responsible for the performance of the group. That group might be called a team, or a crew, or a pod, or a shift, or something else. The name doesn't matter. What does matter is that the way you do your job affects the morale and the productivity of the people on your team.

Robert Sutton is a professor at the Stanford Graduate School of Business. In his book *Good Boss, Bad Boss,* he reviewed the research on the impact of managers. Here's how he summed it up:

"Employees' immediate bosses have far more impact on engagement and performance than whether their companies are rated as great or lousy places to work."

The research is clear. If you're a good manager, you can do things that make your team likely to have both high productivity and high morale. And if you don't? Then, research says, you'll be the reason that people quit. Yes, the old saying is true: "People don't leave companies—they leave [bad] managers." This book is about how you can be an effective and successful manager in a world where changing demographics and technology have reshaped the business landscape.

We live in exciting times, and that means that you'll be facing challenges that your predecessors may not have had to deal with. Many writers on management use the acronym "VUCA" to describe an environment characterized by Volatility, Uncertainty, Complexity, and Ambiguity. Other writers have pointed out that the pace and force of change is probably greater now than it's ever been.

That's all true, but relax. There are some things that haven't changed, and they're important.

WHAT HASN'T CHANGED

Your job is essentially the same as what it was for managers in your parents' and grandparents' generations. And, as far as we can see into the future, you'll be expected to do many of the same things that the managers of previous generations have done.

You must accomplish your mission through the group. People say this in many different ways. They say you must "make your numbers" or "hit your targets" or "achieve your goals." However you describe it, you must do it through your team.

You must help the people who are on your team grow and succeed. Great managers have always been coaches and mentors. They're always looking for ways to help their team members do better in their present job and prepare them for their next move.

You will still be working within an organization. The place where you work has policies and procedures that you need to follow. It has a cadence of meetings and events that stretch across the year. It has a culture, "the way we do things around here," that you must adapt to.

That's pretty general. Let's get a little more specific.

THE MANAGER'S JOB

What is it that you do as a manager? Most of the research and writing for the last couple of decades has concentrated on the subject of leadership. If you wanted to find out what management was, what managers should do, and what makes a good manager, there were precious few places you could look. That's the problem that Google faced.

Google is a fabulously successful company, with offices, managers, and other employees scattered across the world. More than half of their revenue comes from outside the United States. Google is also a company of engineers, and most engineers tend to think that managers are simply not necessary for a company to produce good work. So, Google eliminated managers altogether.

The result was sheer chaos. Communication broke down. Projects ground to a halt. Everyone was frustrated. Google decided that managers were essential to a growing company. They clearly needed managers, but they didn't know if there was much difference between one manager and another. The common-sense answer is clearly, "Yes," but that wasn't enough.

Google is a data-driven company, with very high internal standards of proof for assertions and ideas. They set up a research project called "Project Oxygen" to study managers and what they do.

They started by studying performance reviews and evaluations and company data on team performance to figure out if managers made a difference. The answer was a clear "Yes," but that presented another challenge. The researchers needed to discover what good managers did that their less-successful peers did not do and what the good managers did differently than their less-successful peers.

The research team conducted double-blind interviews with managers from the highest-and lowest-scoring categories on their evaluations. There was a basic script to follow so that the data would be comparable. The research team also reviewed the nominations for Google's Great Manager Award Program and thousands of qualitative comments gleaned from Googlegeist, an annual survey that asks all employees to rate their managers and life at the company.

After reviewing all the data from the interviews and surveys, Google's research identified eight characteristics that were common to the good managers. Here they are in order of importance, as measured by the times they were mentioned in the thousands of surveys.

- A good manager is a good coach.
- A good manager empowers the team and does not micromanage.
- A good manager expresses interest/concern for team members' success and personal well-being.
- A good manager is productive and results oriented.
- A good manager is a good communicator, listens, and shares information.
- A good manager helps with career development.
- A good manager has a clear vision and strategy for the team.
- A good manager has key technical skills that help him or her advise the team.

Here's why I like this research. This is the largest research study of managers that I've seen. Google's research team looked at thousands of managers and evaluated both quantitative and qualitative data. The managers whose performance they evaluated were scattered across several countries, comprised varying personality types. and represented people from many and diverse cultures. And the teams they managed were also made up of people from many cultures.

This is also some of the newest research we have on what makes a good manager. The Google managers whose performance was studied work in an environment very much like the one you work in. Many teams have members scattered across several time zones, even within the US, if not globally.

That makes it excellent for our purposes. No matter what kind of specific training you get in management, you can use the Google findings as a checklist for how you're doing. Let me add one more thing that is not made explicit in the Google material.

I've reviewed several different management-training programs and looked at the ones that my clients use. One characteristic which has become common for all good management training over the last couple of decades is the idea that you should adapt your behavior so that it works best with the person or situation you're facing. My OAR™ tool, which I'll present in the next chapter, will help you learn to analyze and respond to the many different management situations you'll face.

*Adapt your behavior so that it works best
with the person or situation you're facing.*

And I don't mean to suggest you have to do all the adapting work, but once you know why, how, and what, you have the advantage. You can start the process of adaptation, and then you can help your counterpart move toward you.

You must be aware of the personality of the person you're dealing with. Many management training programs cover this using personality assessments such as DiSC or Meyers-Briggs. And these are great, but they don't give you the whole picture.

You must be able to adjust your behavior based on the cultural beliefs of the person you're dealing with, as well. In the next section, I'll teach you how to use my user-friendly 4DCulture™ tool to make sense of situations where differing cultural values are in play.

Whether we're working locally or globally, today we are interfacing with personality and culture.

THINGS THAT HAVE CHANGED

The basic findings from Google's research would be valid twenty years ago. What's exciting is that they're also valid in a world where there will be lots of changes. Here are three important ones:

Teams with remote members are here to stay. The odds are good that you're the leader or a member of a dispersed team now. If you're not, you're almost sure to be before you wrap up your career.

The pace is going to be faster than ever. Everyone says that, but Professor Herminia Ibarra of the INSEAD Business School decided to find out how her students perceived the environment. She did a survey of 173 of her executive-program alumni to look at how things changed in a two-year period, from 2011 to 2013. Her students, executives in companies in many countries, reported major changes in things like the stakeholders they were required to manage and the increase in cross-functional responsibilities. Half reported that there had been significant changes in the business environment in that two-year period. And 42 percent said that the multinational scope of the job had increased.

The teams you are part of will be made up of people from several cultures. You won't have to wait for a change in the "multinational" nature of your job to interact with people who grew up in a different culture. As I outlined in the Introduction, changes in immigration policy in the United States and changes in the global scope of many businesses mean that even if your job is concerned only with the United States, there will be cultural forces in play that you will need to be aware of, support, and leverage for the betterment of your business.

In the next section, I'll introduce you to three powerful tools that will help you be successful as a manager in today's exciting world.

CHAPTER 2

OAR™

Your Multipurpose Tool

Several years ago, I took a road trip along the back roads of the United States with a friend. On the whole, it was a great trip. I got to see parts of the country I'd never seen before, and we had lots of good conversations as we rolled down the highway. But, there was one thing that he did that made me crazy.

He would never stop to look at the map and certainly would never stop to ask for directions. The result was that we'd go miles out of our way when he took a wrong turn. We'd go rolling along down a road that just didn't seem right, with me asking, "Shouldn't I take a look at the map?" The answer was always, "No. I know where I'm going."

I've seen managers act like that, and you probably have, too. They make a wrong decision or get in some kind of trouble, but instead of stopping for a couple of minutes to figure out what's going on or "check the map," they just keep going. Usually, it doesn't end very well.

In this chapter, you are going to learn about a simple but extremely powerful tool that you'll use over and over in all kinds of management situations. It will help you deal with troublesome problems while they're still small and relatively easy to solve. It will help you learn about your people and, even more, develop trusting relationships with them that will help your team perform better. Whether you're working on a project, conducting a meeting, or coaching, this tool will make almost everything you do more effective.

For years, I've worked with managers who were transitioning into unfamiliar situations. Many of them were managers who grew up somewhere other than the United States and who had been transferred here by their companies. Others were people transitioning to a new role, especially from individual contributor to manager.

Those managers who succeeded were young and old, heavy and slim, tall and short, sophisticated and naïve. When I studied them and interviewed them, I noticed a pattern in their communication. I translated their successful behavior into a repeatable technique, which goes by the acronym OAR™.

O is for "Observe." The managers learned to be intensely aware of what was going on around them or in a conversation.

That helped them notice when something wasn't right or wasn't working.

A is for "Ask Questions." This is the equivalent of looking at the map or asking for directions. Questions help you sort out what's actually going on. There's another huge benefit, too. Asking questions can lead you into a conversation. Conversations with team members are the best way we know to build trusting relationships with them. Many conversations naturally start with questions, and asking good questions is a key skill to master for other challenges you will face, like coaching or leading meetings.

R is for "React." This doesn't conflict with the advice you hear from so many people to "be proactive." Instead, reacting is part of adapting your behavior so that it's most effective for the person and situation you're dealing with. As I've said, that's key in almost every management system.

Here's an example of OAR™ taken from real life.

I was on a phone call, coaching a new manager with a Silicon Valley company. I noticed that he was constantly saying "Uh-huh, uh-huh, uh-huh, uh-huh," like he wanted me to speed up. That didn't match the rest of his behavior. He clearly wanted me to share more information with him, and he was reflecting back what I was giving him and telling me it was valuable, but he seemed impatient. So, I stopped the information sharing and asked some questions to verify that he thought what he was getting was valuable.

I verified that he really wanted the information, and so we continued. I tried cutting my sentences shorter and giving him briefer replies, but his impatient behavior continued. I had tried to adapt my behavior, but it wasn't working as I'd hoped, so it was time for more questions.

This time, we were able to come to an agreement. He said that he would cut me short if I was giving him too much information. The questions helped me adapt my style and agree on mutual expectations so that I could ensure he had a better coaching experience overall.

Now, let's unpack the process and look at each of the elements one at a time.

OBSERVE

Observing is about calibrating your antenna so that you're aware of the entire situation that you're in. It might be one on one, like the example I just used, or it might be in a group. Whichever is the case, there are some specific things that you want to watch for.

Sometimes you're having a conversation like I was having with the manager in Silicon Valley, and you notice that behavior is inconsistent. On one hand, he clearly wanted more information, but, on the other, he wanted me to speed up. I needed to find out which was more important, and the only way I could do that was to ask questions.

Watch for times when things simply aren't working. You might be coaching a team member and notice that he or she seems distracted. Sometimes it's more obvious than that. Your team member might have their smartphone out and be checking e-mail while you're talking about how you want them to change their behavior or improve their performance.

Be alert to situations where something changes. If you were sitting in a meeting and somebody suddenly jumped up and ran out of the room, you'd want to find out why that was happening. Most of the time, the cues are less dramatic. You're talking to someone one on one and face to face, and they suddenly change position, leaning forward when, before, they were leaning back, or vice versa. You can watch for body language cues in person, but there are cues even when you're on a phone call. If the other person's tone of voice or manner of speaking suddenly changes, it's something you should find out more about.

Sometimes you'll spot a repeating pattern that happens across several events. Here's an example.

A woman kept coming to her manager and asking for a promotion. Her manager kept saying, "I'm really sorry. I can't do a promotion right now. We have budget restrictions. I just won't be able to do a promotion. I can't, I can't, I can't." The cycle kept repeating, with everyone getting frustrated, until the manager asked a question.

The manager said, "Wait a minute. I know you keep asking for this. Why do you really want a promotion? Maybe there's something else I can do."

That's when the woman shared something she had never said before. "Well, I actually just need more money because I have a disabled child, and I'm a single parent. I need to send my child to a special school so that she's able to really grow and be cared for in the right way."

The manager had just assumed that the woman wanted a promotion for the usual reasons. He might never have discovered the real reason without asking a question.

ASK QUESTIONS

One of the managers I interviewed in the research for this book, summed up the importance of asking questions.

> "I think it's always being inquisitive to understand what makes people tick because we are all so different. We can guess, but it gets you only so far. I think asking helps you understand, and it really helps to establish trust with your direct reports. It shows that you care. It shows that you are really trying to set them up for success."

Consider the examples we just reviewed. Think about my friend on that road trip. You can stop and ask some questions to determine where you are and where you're going, or you can just plow ahead and assume you're right. Sometimes you will be right. But more often you won't, and the consequences can be pretty bad.

Or think about the woman who was constantly asking her boss for a promotion. They were stuck in the same old pattern. The direct report would go to the boss and talk about how she wanted a promotion, and the boss would either tell her why it wasn't feasible because of the budget or talk about ways she could prepare herself to be more promotable. Neither of those things really helped.

But when the manager decided to ask the question about *why* she wanted a promotion, he found something he could do. When the manager understood that his direct report needed financial help more quickly than she was likely to get promoted, he put together a drive to raise money for the special-needs child. He didn't stop helping the woman become more promotable, but by helping her get some financial relief, he took away the urgency to have a promotion happen quickly.

Asking questions helps you learn what's important. But you'll learn more if you ask the right kinds of questions.

The right kinds of questions are what are called "open-ended" questions. An open-ended question is one that can't be answered with a "Yes" or a "No" or with a choice among a limited number of alternatives. Open-ended questions require the other person to share information.

There's another big benefit to asking good questions. Good questions are the gateways to conversations, and conversations are a key way for you to build a relationship and trust with your team members. Building relationships and trust is important, but many managers feel like they just don't have time for conversations.

It's natural to think that asking questions and having conversations will slow you down, but this is really a case of what Stanford professor Bob Sutton calls "going slow to go fast." That's because taking the time to build trust pays big dividends over the long haul. Stephen M. R. Covey wrote a marvelous book about this called *The Speed of Trust*. Here's how he sums up the reasons for taking the time to build trust:

> "Trust always affects two quantifiable variables: speed and cost. Trust equals confidence. When trust goes down in a relationship or a company, speed goes down, and cost goes up. When trust goes up, speed goes up, and cost goes down. Trust always impacts speed and cost."

When people trust you, you don't have to explain yourself or prove yourself as much or as often. When you trust them, you don't have to follow up as often or as vigorously, and you can give more attention to things that move the team forward.

Question-Asking Tip

Culturally, Americans hate dead-air time. We feel the need to jump into a conversation after we ask a question, even if only a second or two has passed. You'll be more successful getting the information you want if you ask your question and then wait for the other person to answer, no matter how long it takes and no matter how uncomfortable you get.

REACT

There's a saying that "no plan survives the first contact with reality." When that happens, you need to react and adjust so you don't continue for fifty miles down the wrong road. Remember Melissa's Management Rule from the last chapter: "Adapt your behavior so that it works best with the person or situation you're facing." When you realize that the behavior you're using isn't working, it's time to react by changing your behavior.

Some of the time, as in the example of my coaching session, you will react in the moment. Sometimes, as in the situation with the woman who kept asking for a promotion, you'll notice a recurring situation or several situations which lead you to believe that you don't have a clear understanding of the situation or the person. Then you ask your questions and modify your behavior.

Sometimes you're reacting to an ongoing situation. You ask questions to determine if you're heading in the right direction. When I have another session with that manager in Silicon Valley, I can ask questions about my pace in advance.

OAR™ is a multipurpose tool for you as a manager because you can use it in so many situations. Keep your antenna up and in scanning mode so you become aware of situations that aren't working, aren't what you expect, or have suddenly changed. Then ask questions to help you analyze the situation and, perhaps, move to a trust-building conversation.

Once you have an idea of what's needed, react by altering your behavior to fit the person and situation.

That's a nice, neat summary, and it makes it seem like this is a quick process. It's not, for a couple of reasons.

It's not neat because we're human beings, and we don't do everything right the first time. It's not quick, because conversations take time. It's also not quick because, many times, there will still be issues or new issues after you've altered your behavior. So, this is not a practice that you go through once and have the right answer. Instead, OAR™ is a tool that you use again and again and again, sometimes several times in a single conversation, just as I did with the Silicon Valley manager.

> **Melissa's Management Rule:**
> *You won't come up with the right behavior or decision just by thinking about it. You need to do something, see if it works, and modify, if necessary.*

OAR™ is a great tool, and it was a great tool even in your grandparents' day. But in the world of the new global manager, it's not just nice, it's essential. It's especially helpful when you're in a situation where cultural forces are in play. That's what we're going to talk about in the next chapter.

CHAPTER 3

CULTURE BASICS

I was starting a new adventure living and working in Germany. Life was pretty good. Except for one thing. Every time we went into a restaurant or a store, my German male friend walked in ahead of me. At first, I was annoyed, but the more it happened, the more upset I got. I was seriously thinking about breaking up with him when I did something I should have done earlier. I asked him about it.

I saw the behavior as selfish and disrespectful, but he thought it was the gentlemanly thing to do. In the culture where he grew up, men walked in front of a woman into, say, a restaurant, to assess the situation and make sure that everything was okay and that there was no threat. From my perspective, growing up in the United States, that seemed backward, but my male friend saw things differently.

The objective reality was the same for both of us. When we went to a restaurant, my friend walked in ahead of me. The problem was that we interpreted that differently. He saw it as the right thing to do. I thought he was being rude, or at least unthinking. In fact, we were both acting normally and politely based on the culture that we grew up with.

As I mentioned in the introduction, culture is what we call the norms, perceptions, and values that drive our behavioral choices. In a world where almost all the people you interact with grew up in the same kind of culture that you did, you didn't have to think about that very much. The challenge in our New Global World is that the people you'll interact with in business may have a totally different set of norms and values from yours.

Normal behavior includes what do we do when we walk into a room. What do we do when we greet people? What do we do when we sit down for a meeting? Who sits where in a meeting room? Cultural norms vary a lot on those simple things and on hundreds of things we don't think about until the moment we realize that things aren't working the way we expected.

I recently visited Dublin, Ireland, for the first time. It was early summer, and the weather was atrocious. It was pouring rain and windy. Living in Arizona, I didn't think to bring an umbrella or appropriate attire, so on my way from the airport to my hotel, I asked my driver if he could make a pit-stop somewhere so I could buy an umbrella. He said,

"Oh, you won't need an umbrella." I wanted to do some touring and enjoy walking the streets of Dublin a bit so I insisted, "Please, I'd like to do some sightseeing. I'll need an umbrella because of the rain." My driver, a native of Dublin, said again, "Miss, you really won't need one . . ." He pulled over at a tourist shop, and I ran in to buy an umbrella. As soon as I stepped outside, the wind blew my umbrella up and inverted it toward the sky. It was at that moment—pouring rain rolling down my face—that I realized my driver meant, "An umbrella will do you no good in this weather."

We all have opinions and assumptions, and those may be true, but they may not apply to all situations. That's why we have to get underneath the obvious behaviors and norms to truly understand the values and attitudes individuals hold.

Germans say they value reliability. Americans will say they value hard work. In India, they'll say family. In Brazil, they say friendliness. To complicate things further, many people grew up in an American household that was strongly influenced by the national culture of their parents. So they're straddling two sets of values (at least). It doesn't mean Germans don't value family or people in Brazil don't value reliability, but values are what we emphasize, prioritize, or understand to be most important.

What does that mean for you as a manager? Let's start with the most important thing you need to know about culture in the workplace.

That was what was happening with my male friend and me. It's what happens to me and what will happen to you over and over again in your life as a manager.

In this chapter, we'll go a little bit deeper into some of the basics of culture. You'll learn about different kinds of cultures and why understanding the cultural forces in play is vital if you want to succeed as a manager. You'll also discover why culture is so tricky and why the OAR™ tool is going to help you again and again.

THREE KINDS OF CULTURE

There are three kinds of culture that drive the behavior of you and the people you work with every day. Behavior is what people say and do. Behavior is observable. As you go about your daily work, behavior is what you work with as a manager. And three kinds of culture drive that behavior.

The culture you're probably most familiar with is **national or ethnic culture**. My male friend was born and raised in Germany. I was born and raised in the United States. We each brought a national culture to our relationship.

There's also **company culture**. Management thinker Marvin Bower characterized this as "the way we do things around here." Company culture drives important decisions, like the kind of people who get promoted and the kind of behavior that's praised or condemned.

You can probably characterize some of the companies you know in terms of their culture. Wal-Mart has a culture that values shaving costs. Apple has a culture of innovation. Ritz-Carlton has a culture of extraordinary service to guests.

In most companies, there are many subcultures. At Apple, the culture of innovation affects every part of the company, but the people in Marketing or Logistics add their own values and norms to the broader company culture.

When you manage a team of people, one of your challenges is to create the culture of your team. The expectations you share, the behavior you reward or tolerate, and team dynamics in general will be influenced by what you do and the way you manage. We'll go into this in detail later in the book, but let's move on with the third kind of culture—one that usually isn't called "culture" at all.

Personality is part of the mix of forces that drive behavior. Sometimes I think of it as "personal culture." You and I and everyone else behave and have certain preferences that have grown out of everything in our life so far. You may prefer to make decisions quickly, while someone else prefers to be more deliberative. You may prefer to send direct, straightforward messages to other people, while some of your colleagues may prefer to be more circumspect.

I represent the three kinds of culture and the way they interact with the following diagram. What makes each person unique is the spot in the center of the diagram where all three cultures overlap.

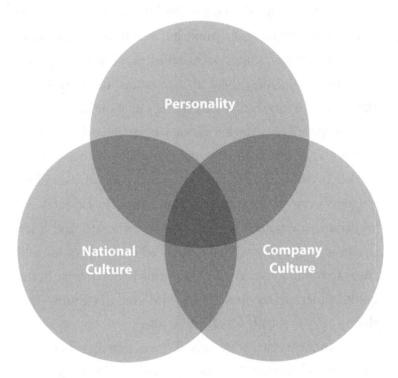

Remember my very first management rule: Adapt your behavior so that it works with the person or situation you're facing. Instruments like DiSC and Meyers-Briggs can help you learn to sort out personality issues. If you use them with your whole team, you also give the team a common language for discussing performance issues driven by personality. The "common language" benefit disappears, though, if you have remote partners who haven't had the same training or you have turnover on the team.

There's another problem with personality instruments if you're in a situation where several different sets of cultural values are in play. When that's the case, you need to use instruments that are normed for each culture. Here's a brief excerpt from the "DiSC Classic Validation Report:"

" ... the behaviors that are perceived as Dominant in one culture may be seen differently in another culture. If we were to measure a person's DiSC style using a language version of *DiSC Classic* that was not developed on the appropriate norm group, the accuracy of measurement and feedback is likely to go down."

Today, you can't count on having team members who are all shaped by the same culture. You need to be sensitive to what's going on and use the OAR™ tool to swim successfully in the invisible waters of culture.

According to some researchers, our national culture accounts for 70 percent of our behavior. I'm not sure if I buy that specific number, but certainly the effects of national/ethnic culture, business culture, and personality influence the way we behave.

WHY IS CULTURE SO TRICKY?

It's obvious that culture is important. Culture is a key driver of behavior, and your job as a manager is to influence behavior so that you, your team, and your team members are more successful. But doing it—and doing it every day—is a lot easier than just saying it.

Culture is tricky because it's invisible. You can't tell by looking at a person what their cultural values are. Remember Karen, whom we described in the Introduction.

If you look at Karen, you would probably assume that because she appears to be Chinese, those are her cultural values. Well, some of them are. But some of her other values come from growing up in the city on the West Coast. She picked up more from the friends she hung around with, and other values came from her education at a small Quaker college. Her worldview is also reinforced by the company where she works today.

If Karen works for you, you can't see any of that. You must observe her behavior, ask questions when she does something you didn't expect, and then react differently than you would if you didn't have any information about what's important to Karen. Yep, it's OAR™.

We also don't talk a lot about our cultural values. We tend to think that our culture is the right way, but we don't think about it a lot. For most of us, our cultural values are internalized and automatic. Think about my male friend and me. We acted and reacted based on our own values. Because those values clashed and because we put off talking about it for a while, negative emotions started to build.

That can happen in the workplace, too. If someone you work with is acting in a way that bothers you, and you don't address the situation (OAR™), it's easy to go on with both of you feeling you're doing the right thing, not understanding the other, and watching the relationship and performance deteriorate.

It's also likely that you'll fall prey to something that social psychologists call the Fundamental Attribution Error. The Fundamental Attribution Error describes our human tendency to leap to a judgment of character based on a single behavior.

Imagine you're in traffic and someone comes up and rides your bumper. You'll probably think something like, "What an idiot!" What you probably won't think is, "I wonder why he's doing that?"

That reminds me of another driving story. A friend of mine was newly here from Mexico, and he was learning to drive for the first time. In taking his permit test, one of the questions he missed was, "What does the yellow traffic light mean?" My friend answered, "Speed up and go through the light," Because, as a passenger, that's what he had seen his American friends do. We all laughed when he told us about missing the question.

But this is a good example where OAR™ would help. Don't assume you know the answer just by observing a situation. Dig in and ask—even some obvious questions. There is less of a chance you'll make a mistake; at least, you'll get a fuller picture.

THE SPECIAL CHALLENGE FOR AMERICAN MANAGERS

Right now, if you're an American manager, you may be thinking that this isn't or won't be a problem for you. After all, America is a multicultural society. Not only that, our companies provide all kinds of diversity initiatives and training. That's true, but I don't think it's the whole story. It seems to me that most American managers don't think that cultural forces create any challenges for them.

Maybe it's our fiercely individualistic national culture that makes us not want to accept that cultural forces exist. We're a large country, with a huge domestic market, and that can lull us into thinking that we don't need to think about cultural forces. That's dangerous.

If you don't recognize the power of the cultural forces in play, you're not going to act to deal with them. You're not going to use OAR™ to observe and ask questions, so you can modify your behavior.

Here's the bottom line: Culture and personality drive a lot of the behavior you'll encounter at work. Everyone you interact with is unique. Their behavior is driven by a unique mix of cultural forces. Your challenge as a manager is to adapt your behavior to their behavior. To do that, you need to think about what cultural forces are in play.

Melissa's Management Rule:
OAR™ is your tool of choice to deal with cultural issues and the surprises a fast-changing business environment will spring on you.

There are so many cultural forces at play and so many situations that it's impossible to prepare to deal with them all specifically. Instead, OAR™ gives you a way to handle situations where behavior is not what you expect. In the next chapter, you'll learn about another tool that will help you sharpen the way you analyze the cultural forces behind the behavior you witness.

As we move from analyzing the US population, demographics, and trends, I'm going to make a shift in language. Part of being a New Global Manager is developing a sensitivity to the feelings and concerns of others. People from the US are not the only people who call themselves "American." People from Central America and Latin America do the same.

I couldn't find a word other than "Americans" for people who live in the United States. So, I coined my own term, which I use in my workshops. The term is "USer." From now on, I will refer to people who live in the US as USers.

CHAPTER 4

4DCULTURE™

Key Cultural Dimensions

A few years ago, I was working with a large German company and helping them deal with global-diversity issues. A senior executive called me into his office and asked me to write the company's global diversity policy.

He said, "You're an expert in the subject, and you know what goes into a policy. Please write one for the company. You have eight weeks."

I thought, *Eight weeks? I can do this in three days. But, okay.*

I went right to work. I wrote the policy, which came out to about three pages. Then I let it rest for a little bit, tweaked it some more, and sent it to an editor so it would be really polished. About a week after our meeting, I sent off the policy, feeling pretty good.

Almost immediately, I got an e-mail back asking me to come right to the executive's office. I thought he might want to praise me for doing such a good job so quickly. When I went into his office, though, he didn't look like he was happy. He held up my work.

"Melissa," he said, "this three-page thing is not a policy. Our policies are at least forty pages long."

He reached behind his desk and pulled out one of the company's policies. Then he went through it with me, showing me all the sections. He outlined everything that needed to be in the policy, and I knew I had a lot of work to do. It might take all of eight weeks, in fact.

What happened? We'd made a classic mistake. We each assumed that the other person had the same idea about what a policy was. I was the expert, and he was an experienced global executive, and we both got it wrong. So will you.

Culture issues are invisible until there's a problem of some kind. The more cultural forces that are in play, the more likely that they'll interact to create a problem. It's inevitable. No amount of planning and preparation can eliminate culture problems. But you've got a tool for that —OAR™—that will help you sort out problems of all kinds, including culture conflicts.

When there's a culture conflict, your challenge is to figure out what's happening. In the situation I just described, part of the reason we got it wrong was that the executive was using German expectations, and I was using American ones. That problem popped up again when we sent the policy around for comment. The Europeans liked it. The locations in Asia thought it was fine. But the USers basically said, "Hey, this thing is too long. No one's going to read it."

That created another problem. When the executive and I got together to discuss it, we decided that the way to deal with the issue was to leave the longer policy the way it was but add my original three-page executive summary in front. That way, people who thought the policy was too long would have something they could read quickly and get the key points.

At the time, I had lots of experience, but I didn't have a specific tool to sort out issues like this. In this chapter, you'll learn more about the instruments that are available and why I decided to develop one myself. I'll introduce you to the tool, which I call "4DCulture™," so you can go into more depth in the chapters that follow.

CULTURE IS COMPLEX, BUT YOUR TOOL SHOULDN'T BE

When you start talking about culture in business, there are an awful lot of things in play. We've already described international culture and business culture and personality and how they interact. The fact is that, no matter who you are, no one else on the planet is the same as you. And, because we don't talk about cultural issues, they're likely to surprise us.

The instruments that I had learned to use to analyze culture in my education and my professional practice embraced every bit of that complexity. Several of them are five-hundred-page-plus academic tomes that are long on theory and short on practical application. The popular "practical" books on culture suggest analyzing as many as a dozen cultural dimensions to figure out how to act.

I limited my system to four dimensions, because research tells us that four is the maximum number of factors a manager can keep in mind in a decision-making situation.

THERE'S MORE THAN ONE CULTURE IN PLAY

There was another problem. All the instruments that I knew of were designed to help you analyze a single culture. If you were an American and were sent to run the Paris office, you could learn about how French people did business differently from you because of their culture. If you were sent to China, you could analyze Chinese business culture and learn how to adapt your behavior.

That's very helpful, but it's not sufficient any longer. We do most of our work in teams, and many of us have team members whose values and expectations were shaped by the culture they grew up in and by, perhaps, even a slightly different business culture that they've been part of.

You don't need a tool to help you analyze a culture. There are plenty out there to help you do that. You need a tool to analyze situations where other people's actions surprise you. And those actions may be based on their cultural backgrounds. You've learned OAR™ to give you a process. The tool I developed, which I call 4DCulture™, will help you use

OAR™ to sort out multiple cultural interactions, conflicts, and surprises at the same time.

4DCULTURE™ BASICS

In the new global business world, you're constantly going to be surprised by situations in which people don't act the way you expect them to. That's what happened with the executive who asked me to write a policy. He expected one thing, and he got something else. When that happens a lot, as it will, you're going to be uncomfortable a lot.

> **Melissa's Management Rule:**
> *You will need to be comfortable*
> *being uncomfortable.*

There will be lots of surprises; you'll be off-balance a lot, but that's not all. No instrument, including 4DCulture™, is going to give you quick, final answers. Instead, you'll come up with ideas that you will try. Some of them will work. Some will not. In many of the situations you'll face as a manager, you will come up with approximate answers and then refine them using OAR™.

My goals for 4DCulture™ were simple. I wanted to give you a tool that you could use in the course of business, where you will have to do your analysis on the fly. I also wanted a tool that was sophisticated enough that you can get to a workable solution as quickly as possible. I began by looking at the available research.

There was a lot of material on analyzing Low Formality cultures. There was a lot of useful material about personality. And there were many authors who had written about business culture. But there wasn't anything that pulled everything together. The literature was helpful, but not sufficient. I needed to do some original research.

I observed working managers in situations in which many different cultural influences were in play. Most of those situations fell into one of two categories. In some of them, a manager was responsible for the performance of a team with members from several different cultures. In other situations, a manager from a country outside the United States was assigned to work here and had to learn to operate effectively in the multicultural environment we have here. I watched what those managers did and what worked and what didn't. I interviewed them.

A pattern began to emerge, and it helped me sharpen my observations and my questions. The four dimensions that we will talk about in 4DCulture™ are the ones which popped up again and again as the cause of surprises and challenges. Here's a brief description of each one:

Time: Rigid Versus Flexible

Some people believe that time can be controlled and that deadlines are fixed. Others believe that you can't control time and that deadlines are flexible. Conflicts here relate to the ways people handle scheduling, punctuality, and deadlines.

Communication: Direct Versus Indirect

Some people say exactly what they're thinking—directly. Others may consider that "brutal." They prefer more indirect forms of communication. Conflicts here often show up in areas of feedback and coaching. They can also affect the mood in meetings.

Thought Patterns: Action Versus Process

Some people want you to share your main point at the beginning of a presentation or e-mail. Others want to hear about your reasoning and process as you lead up to your main point. Conflicts on this dimension can be the difference between winning and losing a sale or approval of a key initiative.

Formality: Low Versus High

USers value a flatter matrix, and we do most of our work as part of a team, however, it's important to call out individual contributors, experts, and even stars in teams. I'm labeling this "Low" Formality. The Japanese, for example, value "High" Formality, working as a team but seeing the authority figure as the expert and decision-maker. Formality is a key determinant of what a person expects from her or his boss.

In each of the following chapters, you'll learn how these differences make an impact on the workplace. But most importantly, please keep in mind that I'm not putting forth a recommendation, I'm only sharing how it is. Either or both ways of being is entirely acceptable, and both will be successful in the workplace. The issue is when people from extreme ends of the spectrum come together and need to efficiently and effectively ramp up a project.

CHAPTER 5

THOUGHT PATTERNS

Action Versus Process

When John's son needed a new bike, he swung into action. John took him down to the local bike shop, let him try a few, and then bought one. The entire time from start to finish was no more than a couple of hours.

Alan did things differently.

When his son asked for a new bike, Alan analyzed his son's needs and launched a research project. He checked out test reports and user comments for different brands and models. He even set up a spreadsheet comparing options. When he was sure he knew what the best bike was, he compared prices at various bike shops and websites. Alan ordered the bike online, and it arrived two days later.

So, who got the best deal? Each father thinks he did a good job. Their sons both love their bikes. Alan is positive that he got the very best price-to-value ratio possible. John knows he picked out a good bike quickly.

John uses an Action thought pattern. He has a goal and immediately goes after it—buying a bicycle—learning about the product and working out details on the fly.

Alan is a Process thinker. He wants to do some homework—weighing pros and cons—before he acts, because he's sure he'll get the best outcome that way.

These two thought patterns crop up all the time in business. Think back to the last project or problem-solving meeting you were in. Some people probably thought there was too much planning and discussion. Others probably thought that more was needed.

Or consider the classic conflict between sales and engineering. Salespeople always seem to want to get on with things. Engineers always seem to want to gather a little more data or refine the work plan or product just a little more.

Almost every business situation will have people who are Action and others who are Process. Look at the graphic of the Thought Pattern Continuum on the following page.

Where do you fall on the continuum? Think about your tendencies. You will probably have a wide range of answers, but where does your behavior fall most of the time? You may get a more accurate assessment by asking several people whom know you well for their opinion.

Thought Patterns									
Action									**Process**
1	2	3	4	5	6	7	8	9	10
Get an idea out there, then figure out how it works					Figure out how it works, then share the idea				
Respond to changes as they come (change is normal)					Plan ahead for the unexpected (change causes stress)				
Allow plans to evolve					Ensure plans are executed				
85% solution, faster					100% solution, slower				

I ask the participants in my classes to assess their behavior. USers mostly rate themselves around 1 or 2. What about some other countries?

"Younger" countries like Australia, New Zealand, Canada, and Israel, along with the US, represent the extreme of Action orientation. Germany, Denmark, the Netherlands, and Russia are the extreme other direction. There, it's common to think about an idea or vision, figure out how it could work, make a plan, and implement it. This is a more Process-oriented thought pattern. India and China are interesting. By nature, they are more Process, but due to more personal, political, and business interactions with the US and the UK, they can adapt well to the Action thought pattern, too.

WARNING: These are only tendencies. More USers are Action than Process, but there are many Process-oriented USers, too. People are shaped by their national culture, but also by their personalities, the places they've worked, and other experiences, the same way that the contacts with the US and UK changed people's tendencies from India and China.

*Every person is different. Use the
tendencies as a starting point, but
treat them as guidelines, not rules.*

Every individual and every situation is different. Your goal should be to discover what behavior works best. Use OAR™ and your understanding of 4DCulture™ to tailor your behavior so that you get the results you want.

OBSERVE

If you grew up in the United States, or if you've worked here for very long, you have probably internalized at least some basic American business-culture values. They include speed and pragmatism. It was USers who developed several forms of Rapid Application Development and the concept of the Minimum Viable Product. Those values are so common in many American companies that no one questions them. In other words, you and the people you work with may not question an Action orientation.

The best companies and the most-effective managers use both processes. One thought pattern isn't better or more effective than the other. The Process approach aims to get a 100 percent solution, even though it will take a little longer. But the idea is that you won't have to come back and retool or service the product to make it work. The Action approach will get an 80 or 85 percent solution but get it faster. A next version or extended service contracts are more common in markets with this thought pattern.

Today the American business press and thought leaders praise the Action approach, but the fact is that great companies use both. When Toyota develops a new car, they alternate emphasis on live trials and thorough engineering to get an excellent product out quickly. The best managers do the same thing.

The most-effective managers adapt their behavior to the person and the situation they're dealing with. Here's an overview of how to decide what Thought Pattern another person prefers so you can adapt your behavior to get the best results.

What kind of "hero stories" do they tell?

Process people talk about the careful planning and research that went into a business success. Action people love the stories about the business plan on a cocktail napkin that resulted in a great company.

What aphorisms or quotations do they use?

Action people tend to divide the world into "Thinkers" (who never take action) and "Doers" (their heroes). They use terms like "analysis paralysis" when colleagues aren't moving fast enough for them. And you'll often hear them say, "We all know what the problem is. Let's get to work." They prefer to go with the flow and solve problems as they appear.

Process people will tell you, "Failure to plan is planning to fail." Or they may suggest, "Plan your work, and then work your plan." They prefer to stick with the plan, and they want to make sure they've refined the plan as far as possible, so they'll often say, "Let's consider a few more options." Or "Calculating our risk is important."

ASK QUESTIONS

The best teams and managers use both Action and Process orientations. Your special challenge as a manager is to ask the questions that help you understand the best way to proceed with your team and how to motivate and engage individuals, leveraging their best qualities.

Here are some examples of questions you could ask:

- What approach would you like to take on this project?
- Do we need a detailed plan to start, or will initial objectives suffice?
- What kind and how much data do we need?
- Should the final report/document be comprehensive or more high-level?
- What kind of detail would you like to see?
- How many slides/pages does it need to be?
- Do you think we need an in-depth training or an executive briefing?
- Do we want a 100 percent solution, or should we create a sample and test it?

- How important are service contracts to our customers?
- What are we staking our reputation on? (Quality, service, etc.)

REACT

There are two action principles you should use with every cultural dimension: 1) Adapt your behavior to what you think will work with the other person. 2) Modify your behavior if it doesn't work. With that in mind, here are some tips for interacting with both Action and Process people:

When you're working with Action people

Make your main point right away. Action people don't want to listen or read through your reasoning and process unless they know what they're evaluating.

Go easy on the details in the beginning. Action people want to get the big picture before they start wrestling with the details.

Expect and encourage collaboration. Action people want to swing into action and work out the process and details with you.

When you're working with Process people

Show the process or reasoning that led you to your recommendation before you share the recommendation. Process people want to understand your reasoning before they evaluate your ideas.

Share the facts and figures you used to reach your conclusion. Process people want to know that you've done your homework.

If you're sending an e-mail, put your main point or action at the end.

CHAPTER 6

TIME

Rigid Versus Flexible

If your company has offices, workers, or partners in countries outside the United States, you probably have some technology that everyone uses. Many companies use the same technology everywhere in the world. What they often miss is that people will use the tool differently, depending on their culture. For an example, think about the simple task of scheduling a meeting.

I did a project for a major software company where we looked at how everyone used the same technology to schedule meetings. When I asked the colleagues in Germany how setting up meetings was working, they said that the technology was great, but they were puzzled by the way their Indian partners reacted when they sent a meeting request.

They could see the Indian colleagues' calendars, and they saw that they said "Yes" to a meeting request even though they were double- and triple-booked. When I talked to the teammates in India, they liked the technology, too. But they were confused by the German behavior because the Germans would sometimes say "No" to a meeting request. Both the colleagues from India and Germany were confused by the USers because USers marked some of the things on their calendar as "Tentative" or entered the meeting with a question mark.

The way that everyone was responding to meeting requests had to do with one of the four dimensions of 4DCulture™. People from Germany have an attitude toward time that I'm calling "Rigid." Look at the chart on the next page to see some of the characteristics.

People from a Rigid culture tend to think that time can be controlled. They tend to do one thing at a time, step by step—what we call "linear" doing and thinking. They don't like interruptions, and they see punctuality as a sign of respect.

In India, time is considered Flexible. So, people's behavior reflects some very different thoughts and beliefs. For them, time is not something that you control—it's something that exists. Instead of doing one thing at a time and working in a straight line, they're more likely to do several things and work on several projects at the same time. People from India not only don't mind interruptions, sometimes they prefer them. Punctuality is not a sign of respect for them, because they see time as more fluid.

In the following graphic, people from Germany would tend to be on the far left of the scale, with people from India on the right. Where would you place yourself?

Time									
Rigid									**Flexible**
1	2	3	4	5	6	7	8	9	10
Time can be controlled									Time exists
Linear doing and thinking									Multidoing & thinking
Prefer no interruptions									Don't mind, even prefer interruptions
See punctuality as a sign of respect									See time as more fluid

Remember that what we're talking about here are tendencies. Not *all* people from India behave as if they are part of a Flexible culture, and not *all* Germans exhibit Rigid tendencies. How about USers? When I ask people in my classes to self-identify where they fit on the scale, US managers tend to be about three or four. They're between the Rigid Germans and the Flexible Indians, but perhaps a bit closer to the Germans.

Remember Melissa's Management Rule:

Every person is different. Use the tendencies as a starting point, but treat them as guidelines, not rules.

Your goal should be to discover what behavior works best. Use OAR™ and your understanding of 4DCulture™ to tailor your behavior so that you get the results you want.

OBSERVE

If you grew up in the United States, or if you've worked here for a while, you've probably absorbed US business culture. American business culture stresses the importance of punctuality. Most of us want and expect our meetings to start on time. We expect people who are going to an appointment to arrive slightly earlier, so they can go in at the proper time. "Time management" is very important.

That's why you're likely to be surprised on the time dimension. When people don't show up on time, when they interrupt you, or when they seem to have a "loose" attitude toward scheduling, you should ask some questions.

Here's an example: Most Flexible cultures are more relationship-based than most Rigid cultures. So, let's say you have two people, one from a Rigid culture and the other from a Flexible culture, who are rushing to a meeting and meet a good friend in the hallway.

The person from the Rigid culture is likely to greet their friend but tell him or her, "I'd love to chat right now, but I've got a meeting. I'll e-mail you, so we can set a time to catch up." The person from the Flexible culture is likely to act very differently. He or she is likely to see the time to stop and chat briefly with their friend as more important than getting to the meeting precisely on time. There's no right or wrong here, but there are differences.

People from more Rigid cultures praise their colleagues who can schedule effectively and stick to the schedule and the plan. People from a Flexible culture are more likely to think highly of colleagues who are close to their families and have large people networks.

ASK QUESTIONS

When you're surprised by the way someone behaves, use questions to discover how you can adapt your behavior to the person and situation. Here are some questions:

- Can I move on, or do you need a minute to make a note?
- Would you like to work sequentially or in parallel?
- My train of thought isn't linear at the moment. Am I making myself clear?
- Would it be alright with you if we had a hard start and/ or stop time?
- Can we agree that meetings will start on the hour?
- What will help us make the deadline?
- Should we meet around the deadline, or would you prefer regular status updates?
- Do we have more to cover, or should I give you/the team some time back?

REACT

There are two action principles that you should use with every cultural dimension. Adapt your behavior to what you think will work with the other person. Modify your behavior if what you do doesn't work. With that in mind, here are some tips for interacting with people who have a different way of thinking about time than you do.

Tips for working with Rigid cultures

Schedules, agendas, and timing are crucial. People with a Rigid sense of time use all the tools available to get the most from their time. They want you to have an agenda for their meetings, and they expect you to honor it. Your Rigid colleagues may be uncomfortable if you end a meeting early.

Organize dates and times for meetings in advance. This helps people with a Rigid sense of time plan their month, week, and day.

Work on one thing at a time; keep it structured. Agendas and checklists are great structure tools. When you have an agenda, go through things in order—don't jump around.

Don't be late to meetings. Remember, people with a Rigid sense of time see punctuality as a sign of respect.

Tips for working with Flexible cultures

Don't force them into your agenda or schedule. This will make them uncomfortable, and they may think you're trying to control them.

Build in regular status updates (daily or weekly). When you are scheduling work, expect to follow up often. Keep checking with Flexible colleagues about details of projects and meetings.

Allow time for socializing and small talk. Most Flexible cultures are relationship-based, and they will be uncomfortable if you get right down to business.

Be prepared for "interruptions" and multitasking.

CHAPTER 7

COMMUNICATION STYLE

Direct Versus Indirect

I like to jog. It's a great way to clear my head after a day of training. It also offers me the opportunity to build relationships with the people in my programs. So, usually at the end of a day of training, I'll suggest going for a jog and ask people if they want to go with me.

The objective reality is that there are only two options. Either someone wants to go jogging with me after class, or they don't. But different people express that in very different ways.

Some people say, "No, I don't want to go jogging," or "Yes, jogging would be great." Sometimes I get a counteroffer. "Well, how about if we go grab coffee instead?" Or, "An hour seems like a long time. What about just going for a twenty-minute walk?"

Sometimes the response doesn't address the idea of going jogging directly. A person might say, "Do you have a fitness center at your hotel?" I might ask my question a couple of times, in different ways, and get several responses before I suss out that they're hinting, "I don't really want to go jogging with you."

The first set of responses is straightforward. You know immediately if the other person wants to go jogging or not. In the last set of responses, the person doesn't actually say what they want. They give me some clues, and I get to put it all together. It might take several back-and-forths for that process to work itself out.

I like to call those communication styles "direct" and "indirect." In the intercultural research by Edward Hall, the language is usually around the culture—low context, and high context. In both cases, there are people in the middle—call them "the bargainers"—who suggest an alternative. They tell me what they would rather do, which also tells me that they don't want to go jogging. Or that they might be willing to go jogging but that they really prefer something else.

Those three groups are a good representation of the way communication styles are spread across a continuum from Direct Communication to Indirect Communication. Review the graphic on the following page.

It turns out that this is a good representation of several different national/ethnic cultures. On the far left of the continuum are cultures like those in Central Europe, Israel, and

Communication Style									
Direct									**Indirect**
1	2	3	4	5	6	7	8	9	10
"Yes" means "I agree"					"Yes" means "I'm listening" or "I understand"				
"No" means "I'm not convinced yet"					"No" means end of conversation or "I'm upset"				
Say what you mean, clarity builds trust					Say what builds the relationship, harmony builds trust				
Conflict should be handled directly					Conflict should be handled discreetly, subtly				

parts of South America. On the far right of the continuum, where communication is more likely to be indirect, are cultures like those in Southeast Asia, India, and parts of Africa. North Americans, the British, and the Australians in my classes have self-identified in the middle—four or five on the continuum.

People whose communication style is more direct believe that you should say what you mean and that you build trust by being clear about things. At the other end of the continuum, people believe that harmony builds trust. They're more interested in maintaining the relationship than they are in expressing an opinion or need. They think it's less important to be explicit than it is to make sure they don't offend me or make me uncomfortable.

People whose style is on the left end of the continuum think conflict should be handled directly. For people whose communication style is indirect, conflict should be handled subtly and discreetly, with a goal of maintaining the relationship.

That's probably a good way for you to decide where you, personally, fall on the continuum. Do you prefer clarity in messages, even if the other person gets uncomfortable? Which is more important to you—the relationship or the mutual understanding? Got it? Now, before you mark your spot on the continuum, here's something interesting about USers. See if this resonates with you.

USers can be very flexible about how they communicate. When it's positive, USers are more direct. We love positive, upbeat, optimistic messages. In fact, some managers refuse to let the people on their teams use the word "problem" because it's negative. Instead, they use a word like "challenge."

When it's time for negative feedback, though, USers slide a little more toward the indirect end of the continuum. US management books suggest that you soften negative criticism with some praise. Now, go back to the continuum, and, instead of one mark, put in two—one for positive and the other for negative.

Obviously, all USers don't communicate the same way. There are USers whose style is very direct and others whose style is at the indirect end of the continuum. The same is true for people from other countries. We're all a mix of many influences that determine the way we behave, including our communication style.

Remember Melissa's Management Rule:

Every person is different. Use tendencies as a starting point, but treat them as guidelines, not rules.

Your goal should always be to discover what behavior works best. Use OAR™ and your understanding of 4DCulture™ to tailor your behavior so that you get the results you want.

OBSERVE

The very tricky part about figuring out communication style is that you're likely to have misunderstandings about what you and another person believe are the meanings of common words. Remember the incident where I wrote the policy for that German company. We both used the same word, "policy," but we had very different ideas of what a "policy" was. One of us had to adapt, and in that situation, it was me. When you're working with a team member or another colleague, you should take the initiative to change so you get the outcome you want.

When I lead classes, I find that the best way to talk about communication style is to talk about words. Let's start with the most basic—"Yes" and "No."

When the person you're dealing with uses a direct communication style and says, "Yes," he or she is telling you that they agree with you. That's not true for people who use an indirect communication style, though. When they say "Yes," it means they're paying attention or they understand. They're not necessarily thinking about "agreement."

On the other hand, if people with an indirect communication style tell you "No," it's likely to mean one of two things. It might mean that they're upset and they're telling you that something you're doing or saying is upsetting the relationship. "No," for them, means that the conversation is over. That's not true for people with a direct communication style. For them, "No" means they're not convinced yet. They still may never agree with you, but they expect to have a conversation first.

The biggest danger in communication style is that you and another person may be saying the same words in the same language and mean different things. Another danger is that messages that a direct communicator uses to obtain clarity might be received by an indirect communicator as something that disrupts harmony or is a challenge. Remember those different responses to my question about going jogging?

Communication Tip

Here's a tip to help you get it right the first time. The words "Yes" and "No" are often and easily misunderstood, so don't use them so much. When someone asks you a question, instead of saying "Yes," and then responding with detail, lose the "Yes." Say only the part of your statement that would come after the comma. That way, your factual statement stands on its own and the possibility of misunderstanding created by "Yes" disappears.

Use the same principle with questions. Instead of asking simple yes-or-no questions, ask more open-ended questions. Instead of asking, "Do you think we'll meet the deadline?" ask an open-ended question like "What is it going to take to meet this deadline?" That way, you're more likely to get helpful information and less likely that there will be a misunderstanding.

That will head off some problems, but it's not going to work every time. So, watch and listen for signals of misunderstanding. Watch for responses that you don't expect. Then move to the second OAR™ step, asking questions.

ASK QUESTIONS

When you're surprised by what someone says or does, use questions to discover how you can adapt your behavior to the person and situation. Here are some questions.

- Shall we get straight to the point here?
- What kind of feedback would you like to hear?
- Where are you from?
- I grew up on the East Coast, and we don't sugarcoat things. Are you okay with that?
- What area of the business do you work in? (Engineering will be more direct, marketing perhaps less so.) Would you like to hear what worked and what could be improved?
- How would you like to work together?
- What kinds of advice or help would you like to receive from me?
- Would you like to be mentored or coached? (Told or asked.)

REACT

There are two action principles that you should use with every cultural dimension. Adapt your behavior to what you think will work with the other person. Then, modify your behavior if what you do doesn't work. With that in mind, here are some tips for interacting with people who have a different communication style.

Tips for Working with People
Who Use a Direct Communication Style

State what needs to happen directly. Check for understanding.

Give explicit feedback, even if it's negative. If you grew up in North America, or you've absorbed American business culture, you will probably find it hard to be direct about negative feedback. It can create problems if you're not direct with people who have a direct communication style, because they will not understand that you mean the feedback to be negative.

When you're dealing with someone with a direct communication style, you should be direct. Say what you want or what you like specifically. If you don't want something or don't like something, say that directly. Remember that people with a direct communication style believe that clarity builds trust. Strive for clarity by being direct.

Tips for Working with People Who Use an Indirect Communication Style

Be very careful about giving feedback to someone with an indirect communication style. Be sure to do it one-on-one and privately. Demonstrate that you value your relationship with them.

If you're giving negative feedback to someone with an indirect communication style, it's usually a good idea to incorporate a little praise.

People with an indirect communication style can be offended by direct communication, so to adapt, you must be subtler and more discreet. Let them know what you want or like, but don't say it directly.

CHAPTER 8

FORMALITY

Low Versus High

Teaching classes is a great experience for me. I get to meet lots of interesting and competent people and learn even more about a subject I love: how cultural forces impact the way we do business. In every class, I learn a little more as participants share their experience and insights. For example, a manager from France told me the following story that I can now share with you.

The French manager was responsible for several development teams, one of which was in Mexico. That team was having problems solving a technical issue. When the French manager discussed things with the team lead in Mexico, it was clear that the team lead understood the problem very well. So, the manager from France asked, "In our next team call, could you please present the problems, so we can all discuss them and try to solve them?" The team lead agreed.

On the day of the call, he was out sick. He had always communicated often with the French manager, but now communication stopped. The manager tried to reach his direct report from Mexico but never could manage to connect. Then the manager from France discovered that his colleague had left the company. The manager was totally shocked.

He had had a good relationship with his Mexican colleague. So, he didn't understand why the man had left the company, not returned his calls and e-mails, and had not said anything about leaving. So, he did a little digging.

The French manager discovered that, while he thought having the Mexican team member explain things to the whole team while he was present was just a way to get at the problem, his direct report took it very differently. Looking through the Mexican team member's cultural lens, explaining the details of the problem in a meeting where the boss was present was not the right thing to do. He assumed it made his boss look like a bad manager, if the French manager was not the one to deliver the bad news himself. And, therefore, he assumed the manager was setting him up to fail or to take the hit for the problems in the project.

It was a classic case of something we've seen before. The manager from France was acting based on his culture, but the direct report from Mexico was evaluating it based on his culture.

What was going on was a mismatch on the cultural dimension that I call "Formality." Loosely based on the intercultural research in Individualism vs. Collectivism, Formality is a little tricky because we orient ourselves socially in two different directions. We orient ourselves with the way that we relate to the groups or teams that we're part of. And, especially in business, we orient ourselves in our relationship to the people above and below us on the org chart. Look at the graphic below.

Formality									
Low									High
1	2	3	4	5	6	7	8	9	10
Uses "I" statements							Uses "We" statements		
Concerned with individual achievements						Concerned with group achievements			
The individual takes initiative						The boss takes initiative			
I can decide on direction and ask for approval/help					The boss decides on direction and tells me what to do				

On the left side of the graphic are cultures that are Low and less hierarchical. The right end of the graphic is the opposite of that. I call those High cultures, and their hierarchy is more important. Here's how that works:

People with Low Formality tend to use "I" statements, while those with a High use "we" statements. People from a Low Formality culture are more concerned with individuals and individual achievements, while those from High

Formality cultures are more concerned with group achievements and being seen as a part of the group.

Psychologist Harry Triandis demonstrated the difference in an interesting way. He asked people from different cultures to describe the same aquarium scene. The people from the Low Formality cultures (or as he described, "Individualistic") described the individual items in detail but rarely mentioned the relationship between them. People from High Formality cultures (or "Collectivistic") saw the same scene differently. They described the entire scene, including the relationships between the individual items. And that's only one difference between the two cultures.

In Low Formality cultures, the individual takes the initiative. But in High Formality cultures, the manager takes the initiative. In Low Formality cultures, team members can decide what to do and ask the manager for approval or help. That's not true for High Formality cultures. There, the manager makes the decision on direction and tells the team members what to do. He or she may describe how to do the work in great detail.

The French—and Western Europeans generally—are more toward the Low Formality side of the graphic, around three or four on the scale. Mexican culture is at the other end of the High Formality scale, around nine or ten. That difference was at the root of the problem above.

For people with High Formality, it's not appropriate for a team member to challenge the team leader or make the team leader look bad. And, that's what the Mexican team member thought he was going to do if he described a problem in front of the whole team with his manager present.

The outcome of that situation was extreme. Usually, people don't leave a company because of a Formality issue. But I've heard other managers from other Low Formality cultures describe the situation of asking one of their team members to outline technical issues on a project to the manager's boss when the manager was present. Even if the team member has agreed to explain the issues, they often won't do it when faced with that culturally difficult situation. It's an example of why mastering the cultural dimensions will help you be more effective in creating a great working environment.

People from Central America, India, and China are more likely to be at the far end of the High Formality scale. A little bit to their left, around seven or eight, are some of the Eastern European cultures, like Romania or Moldova. Scandinavian and Central European cultures are more toward the other end of the scale, leaning more Low Formality. At the far left of the scale is where you'll find USers.

In my classes, USers characteristically identify themselves as one or two on the Formality scale. When USers have a manager from a High Formality culture, they may feel micromanaged, while the manager feels that she or he is appropriately and proactively involved with the USers' work.

Place yourself where you think you fit on the continuum. As in all the other cultural-dimension chapters, we're talking about tendencies here. There are managers who grew up in the United States and who act with more High Formality. And there are people from Mexico or France who act differently than their national/ethnic origin would suggest.

> ### Remember Melissa's Management Rule:
> *Every person is different. Use the*
> *tendencies as a starting point, but*
> *treat them as guidelines, not rules.*

OAR™

If you grew up in the United States, or if you've worked in the US for a while, you've probably absorbed some of American business culture. American business culture is strongly individual. We value assertive and confident behavior. We see taking initiative as a good thing. We are used to freewheeling discussions where it's common for someone to talk to the boss directly.

That business culture has served the US well, but if you're the manager of a group today, you're going to work with people who come from a very different Formality level who will act differently. The best way to determine someone's Formality level is to listen.

People with more Low Formality use "I" statements a lot. They talk about their own individual achievements or the individual achievements of other team members.

People from High Formality cultures tend to use "we" statements. That's a clue to their Formality level, but it can be a trap in the United States. That's because US managers have been trained in the last twenty years or so to use a lot of group language. It's common to hear a boss from the United States, with Low Formality, refer to the group as "we." So, that word can be a clue, but you should also pay attention to a couple of other things.

Pay attention to the silence. Men and women with Low Formality expect to jump into conversations and challenge authority. They love classic brainstorming sessions, where everyone is expected to pitch in and throw out ideas, and problem-solving meetings where team members challenge each other and their boss. On many teams, though, there are people who don't participate in that kind of activity.

Those people are likely to be acting from High Formality. They may think that it's inappropriate to stick out as an individual. They won't do things that make it look like they're trying to stand out from the group.

The basic rule for OAR™ is the same as it is for the other social dimensions. When someone acts in a way that you don't expect, stop and Observe. What did they do or not do that surprised you? When another person's behavior doesn't match your expectations, it's time for the second part of OAR™. It's time to Ask Questions.

ASK QUESTIONS

When you're surprised by what someone else does, use questions to discover clues about how you can change your behavior so it's more effective for that person and that situation. Here are some questions.

- What is the role of a leader?
- Shall we have regular status updates?
- Would you prefer to let me know if and when you need help?
- How do you see your role on the team?
- Would you like to take the lead in a few meetings?
- Shall you and I speak before the meeting and I'll relay the information to the team?
- How shall we address problems or conflict?
- What can we do to improve teamwork?
- Should we go around the room and hear from everyone?

React

The two action principles for this dimension are the same as for all the others. Adapt your behavior to what you think will work with the other person in this situation. Modify your behavior if what you do doesn't work. To help you get it right faster, here are some tips about how to work with people who have a different Formality level.

Tips for Working with People Who Have Low Formality

Ask for advice from experts on the team. People with Low Formality tend to see teams as a group of individual experts.

Rotate leadership responsibilities to keep team members engaged. You don't need to have all the answers or act like you're in charge all the time. Team members who have Low Formality expect to take the lead in areas where they're expert.

Agree on priorities as a group, and then give autonomy to individuals to handle issues. Be available to support as needed. Expect people to come to you with ideas or issues.

Reward individuals, and promote them within the team and beyond.

Tips for Working with People Who Have High Formality

Lead with authority. People with High Formality expect the manager to be in charge and make decisions. Get consensus, but make the ultimate decision yourself.

Give clear instructions, and assign tasks to individuals. Team members with High Formality expect you to get into the details. Talk to individual team members, and ask them what you can do to support them.

Don't put team members on the spot. People with High Formality hate being singled out from the group, even if it's for praise. Praise and reward the team.

CHAPTER 9

KEEP ASKING AND LEARNING

"Getting it wrong is usually part of getting it right."

I don't know who said that first, but it's certainly true. You won't learn to be a good manager without getting it wrong a lot. When I tell people that in class, I almost always have someone ask me about a time I got it wrong. When that happens, I recall a great learning experience that I think of as "negotiating with the Chinese ambassador's wife."

I was living in Berlin at the time, where I was only one of a few people doing intercultural communication coaching. One of my corporate clients referred me to the new Chinese ambassador. He was taking up a post at the Chinese embassy in Berlin, and his wife contacted me about doing some coaching sessions on German culture, lifestyle, and business practices.

When I presented the proposal and the cost, the ambassador's wife immediately said that it was too much. That surprised me, because I knew that my prices were fair, given the market in Germany, but I offered to change the proposal. I suggested reducing the amount of time we would spend together and removing a few of the support materials I had planned to deliver. The result was a lower price.

The ambassador's wife was very firm. She wanted the same time and materials for a reduced price.

I really wanted to do the project. I was honored by the prospect of working with the Chinese embassy, and I thought it might help me get other business in diplomatic circles. With that in mind, I agreed to reduce the entire project by 10 percent. When the ambassador's wife told me that that was entirely unacceptable and that my offer was too high, I decided she was a difficult person and that I really didn't want to work with her. So, I told her I was sorry that I couldn't reduce the price any more. We parted ways, and I thought I had lost the proposal.

About a week later, I received an e-mail from the ambassador's wife saying that she and her husband would like to hire me for a series of coaching sessions. The e-mail made it sound as if we had never had the previous interaction, and I was confused. So, assuming this was some sort of strange game, I wrote back with a price that was 20 percent higher than my original offer (since at this point I didn't really want the project anyway). She countered with a price that was the same as what I had initially offered in our first discussion.

I was still puzzled—she wasn't getting a discount. I decided to do the project, and everything worked out very well! The ambassador's wife cooked an elaborate meal for lunch, thanked me profusely after the session, and went on to recommend me to others. But I almost lost the opportunity because I had violated some of my own rules.

When you know you're going to be in a situation with someone whose culture is different from your own, you should do some homework. The 4DCulture™ tool will help you. If I had done my homework, I would have learned something important. In the US, we usually strive for a win-win outcome in negotiations. But, in Chinese culture it is a common belief that someone must win, and someone should lose a negotiation. Even if it's only at face value.

Use what you know about the person and their culture to decide how you are going to interact with them. You may not get it right the first time, but you're more likely to succeed if you do a little homework. I hadn't done that. I had never negotiated with someone from China before, but I went ahead without doing my homework. That was my first mistake.

When you're interacting with another person and you're surprised by what they do, you need to stop and ask questions, so you can decide how to do better. That's what the OAR™ tool is for. In this situation, I didn't do that. Instead, I pressed on just like I was dealing with a USer or a European. It could have all gone really badly, but I got lucky.

However, you can't count on getting lucky. You've been introduced now to the 4DCulture™ tool to help you analyze the cultural forces that may be in play. And, you should already be using the OAR™ tool for situations when you're surprised by the way other people act. In this chapter, we'll investigate how you can use those tools more effectively and how you can deepen your understanding of cultural forces. Here's a rule to guide you:

Melissa's Management Rule:

No one is the same as you. You will constantly be surprised by the way people behave, so you will always be in learning situations.

NO ONE IS THE SAME AS YOU

Alfred Tennyson wrote, "I'm a part of all that I have met." That's true, and it's also true that you are the result of everything you've experienced. What makes you unique is how all the things that have shaped you come together. Take a look (again) at the following diagram.

Each of the circles represents one of the major clusters of the forces that have shaped each one of us. You, and everyone else, are shaped by the national or ethnic culture that you're part of. The place where you work, even the places you have

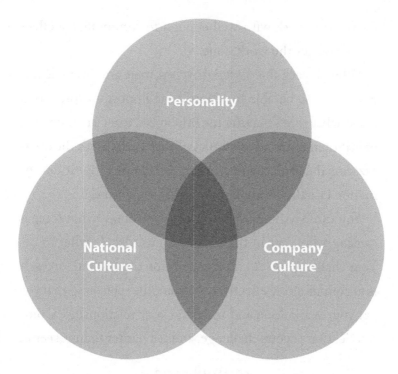

Personality

National
Culture

Company
Culture

worked, help determine the way you act in a business setting.
And then, there's personality.

Your personality's shaped by many things. Certainly, it's
shaped by your parents and your formative experiences.
Teachers and mentors and coaches have influenced the way
you act. And, there are researchers who think that biochemistry is part of the mix, along with genetics.

That part of the diagram where the three circles overlap
is the unique you. The reason we are different from each
other is that we all have a different mix of experiences and
influences. Your challenge as a manager is to understand the

people you work with well enough to communicate effectively and get the work done.

When I teach this material in class, there are always people who want to be able to identify the important force. Is it personality that's making the other person act a certain way, or is it their national or ethnic culture? Perhaps it's the organizational culture we're working in. Here's a tip: it doesn't matter. Usually all are in play at the same time.

You can have a marvelous discussion about what force is causing what, but in the end, you must decide what to do. Your challenge isn't to pin the name on the cultural forces. It is to communicate effectively with another person so that you get your work done and maintain your relationship. Communication is your challenge, and it's harder than it seems.

COMMUNICATION

Communication can seem simple, especially when the two people who are communicating are speaking the same language. But when you analyze communication, it turns out to be quite complex.

Our messages go through filters, especially when there's more than one culture in play. The sender sends an intended message, and it goes through a set of filters. The receiver receives it and sends a message back, and it also goes through a set of filters. That means that the message that's received on either end may not be what was intended by the sender.

Look at the diagram below. It illustrates the process and just a few of the potential barriers to communication.

Barriers to Communication

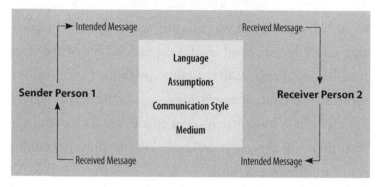

Language can be an issue. We can speak the same language and have a very different idea of what particular words mean. Words may mean different things to different people.

The assumptions we bring to the communication matter, too. Recall the incident when I wrote the policy for my German client. His assumption was that a policy is a forty-page, detailed document. Mine was that a policy was a two- or three-page guideline. The tricky thing about assumptions is that we rarely state them.

The medium we use affects our communication. There's one dynamic if I'm communicating with one of my team members and we're sitting across from each other, but quite a different thing if we're having the same conversation on the telephone. Then we must make do without the visual cues we have when we're face-to-face. And e-mail is a different dynamic from both face-to-face and telephone communication.

The issue of communication style can get in the way. What's entirely acceptable to one person may be seen differently by another. I was recently working with a leadership team that spanned several countries. One of the team members sent an e-mail to another without a greeting or a sign-off, just content consisting of an update and a request. He thought it was entirely okay, efficient and clear, but she thought it was aggressive and rude. Was it? The sender didn't think so. The receiver did.

That's the problem with many communication issues: there's more than one truth. Your challenge as a manager is to sort it out so the teammates can continue working with each other without communication issues, stereotypes, or resentments getting in the way.

Let's take a minute to think about stereotypes. Racial or ethnic stereotypes can be a problem, but we usually spot them quickly enough and have some idea of how to deal with them. A subtler challenge is a prejudice about time management, cultural differences, intelligence levels, or analytical skills.

If you're feeling intimidated by this, don't be. Every day, managers all over the world make this work, and you can, too. Your basic tools are OAR™ and 4DCulture™.

OAR™—Observe, Ask Questions, React—is a powerful tool you can use in all kinds of situations. That doesn't mean that you'll do it all the time. Sometimes you'll do what I did with the Chinese ambassador's wife. You won't understand, but you'll plow ahead anyway. We all do that. In the beginning, you'll have to think about using the OAR™ tool, but if you keep working on it, it will become instinctive.

> ### Management Tip
> The 4DCulture™ tool gives you a way to make your first determination about how you're going to act and then to ask the questions and analyze the situation so that you do better. You'll find, often, that the process is progressive. Your first analysis won't get it quite right, your second analysis will do better, and your third will improve on that.

OAR™ and 4DCulture™ are powerful tools. But it doesn't matter how powerful a tool is—you must be able to use it. In the next section, we'll talk about how you apply OAR™ and 4DCulture™ in a variety of real-world situations.

CHAPTER 10

APPLICATIONS SECTION INTRODUCTION

In the last twenty years, I've visited more than forty countries for the first time. It was always an exciting experience, even though it was also always a little bit scary. Before my first visit, I'd do some research to learn about the place where I was going and the people I would meet and the culture I would experience. That helped a lot, because when I got to the new place, I could make some sense of what was happening and how people were acting. The research and preparation I did before my trip made the experience more productive and less uncomfortable. But I was always at least a little uncomfortable.

It was a new situation, and I had to learn to adapt to it. And, no matter how much research I'd done in advance, I really learned about the place I was visiting only by being there and experiencing it. That's how it will be for you as a global manager.

This book, and other books you read, will help you recognize situations and figure out how you want to interact with them. You'll also learn from more experienced managers. Any formal management training you have will help, too. But you still must learn how to be a good manager on the job.

In fact, most management-training experts say that, by the time you have mastered the work of managing, you will have learned 10 percent from books and articles and formal classes. You'll get another 20 percent from other people, usually other managers. But you'll learn a full 70 percent on the job.

Don't discount the reading and classes because of the low percentage. Classes and books like this one should give you practical models and tips that you can apply so you learn faster and avoid common rookie-manager mistakes. The final chapters in this book are designed to help you get the maximum amount of value out of your on-the-job learning. Before we get to the chapters in this section, though, let's take a couple of minutes to review the important things we've covered so far.

THE BASICS OF BEING A GOOD MANAGER HAVEN'T CHANGED

There are a lot of things about the world today that are different from previous decades and generations. There will be even more changes throughout your career. Even so, good managers today and good managers tomorrow will do some of the things that good managers have always done.

In the Becoming a New Global Manager chapter, I introduced you to the Google research on the eight things that the best managers do. Here's that list again:

- A good manager is a good coach.
- A good manager empowers the team and does not micromanage.
- A good manager expresses interest/concern for team members' success and personal well-being.
- A good manager is productive and results-oriented.
- A good manager is a good communicator, listens, and shares information.
- A good manager helps with career development.
- A good manager has a clear vision and strategy for the team.
- A good manager has key technical skills that help him or her advise the team.

Your challenge is to do those things in a New Global context. Depending on your specific situation, you'll do the same things, but you may do them differently than a manager of twenty years ago or a manager in a different situation.

THE NEW GLOBAL ENVIRONMENT IS DIFFERENT

Because of changes in US immigration law and in business, the New Global environment is different. American attitudes have changed, too. Once it was common for people to give up their cultural traditions and language to assimilate into the American "melting pot." Today people keep those traditions while simultaneously being part of American culture. The important difference, for you, is that there are more cultural forces in play than was true for previous generations.

There are always at least three sets of cultural forces in play. National or ethnic culture drives your actions and the actions of the people you interact with. For people who grew up in the United States, this is often the national or ethnic culture of their parents. Your company culture has an impact, too. And, every person you interact with also has a personality. That personality is partially the result of their experiences growing up but also of things we can't identify specifically.

Change is constant. US businesses are increasingly global, and more and more companies from other countries are doing business here. Technology is also a major force driving change. Technology enables us to communicate, almost instantly, with people anywhere in the world, and it has sped up the pace of business and change.

All those forces have created a business environment that is constantly in flux. Beyond the minimum, you can't plan for

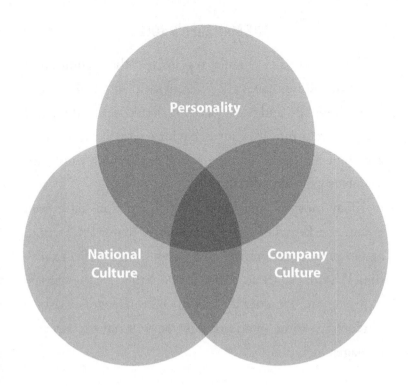

what you'll face. So, you must learn how to adapt. OAR™ and 4DCulture™ are your tools of choice to sort out what's happening and find something that works.

This final section of the book has three chapters that will give you some ideas about how to use your understanding of the New Global environment and the OAR™ and 4DCulture™ tools to do a better job as a manager. They'll give you some idea of common situations that you'll confront, and common ways that you can use OAR™ and 4DCulture™ to find the right solution as quickly as possible.

THE MANAGER'S ROLE

In the Formality chapter, you learned that people from different cultures have very different ideas about what managers should do and how decisions should get made. You'll learn how to modify your behavior to do a better job of accomplishing your team's mission and helping your team members grow and develop.

Today, most routine administrative functions have been automated. So, what's left for a manager to do? Interaction, empowerment, connection, engagement, and conflict resolution. We still call these "soft skills," but they are the hardest to master and the ones that set the best managers apart.

Here are some of the things you will have to do as a manager, including:

- Advocating for and creating visibility for your team.
- Protecting your team.
- Managing up on behalf of your team.
- Getting out of the way so your team feels empowered to be more autonomous.
- Being available and approachable to give feedback and coach.

You will do all those things, but you will do them somewhat differently, depending on the people and situation you face. You will do them more effectively if you understand what individual team members expect from you in your role as manager.

PRACTICAL APPLICATIONS

As a manager, you will spend most of your time on people issues. In the chapter on Practical Applications, you'll learn important things about four high-leverage tasks. They are:

Feedback
Coaching
Presentations
Meetings

We'll discuss the basics of these four critical tasks. You'll learn how 4DCulture™ and OAR™ will help you do a better job.

MANAGING TEAMS

This is where it all comes together. In this chapter, you'll learn about what makes effective teams and effective team culture. You'll get some specific tips on managing meetings and especially virtual meetings.

I like to think of this book as your guidebook to the world of managing in the New Global business environment. In each of the chapters that follow, you'll find critical things you should be aware of and how to apply the tools of the New Global Manager to the real-world situations you'll face on the job.

CHAPTER 11

THE MANAGER'S ROLE

As a manager, you're expected to balance your individual-contributor role—that is, your daily tasks—with your manager duties. In your manager role, you are the person most responsible for the productivity and morale of your team. The people you manage expect you to advocate for them and their careers, create opportunities, and help them move up and on. You really don't have a choice about that.

One of the *Merriam-Webster Dictionary*'s key definitions for the word "role" is: "a socially expected behavior pattern, usually determined by an individual's status." Your role is what the people around you expect of you. To help you understand what that means for you as a manager, I'd like you to do a short exercise.

There are no right answers for this exercise. It's not a test of any kind. I'd like you to think about the answer to this question: "What makes a good manager?"

I don't know what you thought or what you wrote down, but I can tell you some things about your answer. Some of what you expect from a good manager is based on your national or ethnic culture. Some of what you expect is the result of your personality and experiences. And some of what you expect is based on your organizational or workplace culture. Here's a reminder of something we've discussed previously.

Melissa's Management Rule:
You make choices and decisions based on your culture, but people evaluate your actions based on their culture.

In other words, someone who grew up in a different national or ethnic culture may expect something different from you. Ditto for someone with a different personality or work experience.

Melissa's Management Rule:
No one is the same as you. You will constantly be surprised by the way people behave, so you will always be in learning situations.

In this chapter, you'll learn about common issues with your role as a manager that are driven by cultural forces. I interviewed managers from all over the world working in the US, and they consistently described a manager's role in American business culture as collaborating with team members and encouraging suggestions and participation from everyone. That works especially well when everyone has the same expectations, but that's not always the case.

Tom was born, raised, and educated in the US. Before he joined his present company, he worked for US companies, and he had US managers. It should be no surprise that he imagines a manager's role as being open to ideas and suggestions from team members.

Recently he joined a Japanese company, and his new manager has just relocated here from Japan. Tom manages his US team the way he's always managed and been managed. The team culture is collaborative. They like to move quickly, making decisions on the fly. It's a dynamic environment.

Tom's manager, Haruto San, sends lists of to-dos to Tom every Monday morning. He then follows up at the end of the week by e-mail to see what's been done. There are no one-on-ones, no team meetings, and especially no discussion on what, how, or when. Tom perceives it as just orders, and that's not what he's used to.

Tom's feeling demotivated and frustrated. He doesn't believe Haruto San is bringing him into the process or the decision-making. It's not normal or comfortable for Tom to just get marching orders. He hasn't worked his whole career just to execute on demand without discussing strategy, impact on the business, or relationship to the customer.

If Tom can step back for a moment, he will be in the Observe part of OAR™. He is witnessing behavior that, in this case, doesn't agree with him. Tom's next step should be to Ask some questions (the second step in OAR™) to understand the situation better and learn what's behind Haruto San's behavior. Is it personality? Is it culture? Is it a personal conflict? Using OAR™ will, hopefully, give him more answers and allow him to move toward an effective solution.

Because Tom's manager grew up in a different culture, the first thing Tom should ask is: "Does this fit Japanese culture?" Another way to ask that might be: "Is this normal for Japanese managers?" He may want to consider speaking to some other subordinates or former colleagues of Haruto San in Japan and reading up on Japanese business practices.

In this case, when Tom reviews the cultural dimensions in 4DCulture™, he decides that the Formality dimension is most helpful for this situation. Tom learns that Haruto San is acting like most Japanese managers. On the Formality scale, Tom is far to the left, valuing individual initiative, like most USers. Haruto San is far to the right. He values a strong hierarchy and subordination to authority and the group. He understands his role as giving clear direction to Tom.

At this point, Tom has two basic options for how he can React (the third step in OAR™). He can adjust his expectations, or he can try to change the situation. Tom decides to send an e-mail to Haruto San, politely offering his analysis of the situation and asking Haruto San to manage him in a more collaborative way. That only seems to make things worse.

Tom is surprised again. He goes back to the 4DCulture™ dimensions and discovers that American and Japanese cultures are far apart on the Communication dimension as well as on Formality. Tom values simple, clear communication where his messages are accepted at face value. Haruto San prefers more indirect communication, where much is read between the lines.

So, what should Tom do? So far, he has used OAR™ effectively. Each time he has been surprised by what happened, he stopped and attempted to figure out what was really going on. This is an extreme example because Tom and Haruto San are far apart on two dimensions. But it's realistic because, as with most people issues, there's no quick fix.

Eventually—understanding that things are not going well with Tom—Haruto San brings in a third party. I explain to the whole team the expectations between cultures and facilitate a discussion on individual needs and ways to move forward successfully. The whole team benefits from the time together discussing how communication can improve, Haruto San "saves face" as it was his idea to have the externally facilitated meeting, and Tom feels positive about the action items they take out of the coaching session.

I know about this situation because Haruto San brought me in to help sort out the communication issues. In my experience, everyone usually knows when there are problems, but sometimes they don't know what to do about it. Tom understood OAR™, so he had a tool to work with from his side, but Haruto San did not.

Haruto San knew there were problems, and the only option he thought he had was to bring in an expert facilitator. He reached out to HR, and they reached out to me. This is an extreme solution, but it's sometimes the right one for a difficult problem.

Most of the problems you will encounter as a manager have a solution. Some may have a solution that's quick and easy. In my experience, most issues and misunderstandings have to do with how people communicate with one another.

Relationships and building trust are critical, and they won't happen either all at once or quickly. You'll be a more effective manager if you concentrate on making some progress every time you interact with either your boss or other team members. The most important issues you will confront as a manager are people issues. One of the managers I interviewed put it this way:

> "A lot of managers hardly do any people management. But if you can't do 50 percent or more people management, I think you are not in the right job."

Another important part of people management is "managing up." It is your responsibility to understand your boss's preferences and to help her or him succeed. You must be able to negotiate and advocate for what your boss and team need, act as a bridge, and keep the communication flowing.

Tom will be a more effective manager if he chooses to adapt and at the same time make his expectations clear so that his boss and team members have the opportunity to meet him halfway. Remember the very first management rule we introduced in this book.

Melissa's Management Rule:

Adapt your behavior so that it works best with the person or situation you're facing.

Using OAR™ will help you adapt to situations that surprise you. 4DCulture™ gives you tools to analyze situations where cultural forces of all kinds are in play so that you can adapt your behavior more effectively.

CHAPTER 12

PRACTICAL APPLICATIONS

How will you spend your time when you're back on the job?

The Center for Management and Organizational Effectiveness surveyed managers across North America and discovered that most of them spend most of their time working with other people. That includes meetings of all kinds and one-on-one time with team members. In fact, most managers spend only an hour and forty-five minutes a day on their own tasks and projects.

This chapter is about getting the most value you can from your people-management time. I've identified four activities that will offer you ways to make a big difference in individual and team performance. And if you master the art of doing them well, you will save time, scale yourself as a manager, improve your own brand or image in the organization, and impress your manager. The areas are:

Feedback

Coaching

Presentations

Meetings

You'll learn why each one is important, insights and models to help you do it well, and how OAR™ and 4DCulture™ can help you give feedback, coach, make presentations, and hold meetings even more effectively. Let's start with an activity that most new managers dread—giving negative feedback. If feedback is positive, it's easy, but when it's necessary to stop, change, or improve something, that's when delivering feedback gets tricky.

FEEDBACK

If you're worried about having "difficult conversations" with a team member, you're in pretty good company. Most effective managers felt that way until they learned how to give feedback constructively. They also found that they could be much more effective if they created a "culture of feedback"— meaning they set the expectation upfront that feedback is a normal and healthy part of teamwork. That starts with knowing what feedback is.

Let's say that one of your team members is late with a project report. That affects team performance. Perhaps other team members can't do their job, or perhaps it means that you're late sending your own project report to your boss. No matter what the reason, it's something that keeps the team from performing at its best. Your job, as a manager, is to do something about it. That something is called "feedback."

Feedback is the process of providing information or observations about something that's already been done and needs to be done differently (or in the case of positive feedback, continued) in the future.

Feedback is important for two reasons: 1) When your feedback helps someone improve their performance, team performance improves, too. 2) People don't want to do a bad job or let their teammates down. Your feedback helps them achieve better results and maintain their good standing in the organization. They feel better about their work overall. Their morale and the morale of the team improves. Everybody wins.

Delivering Effective Feedback

Before you can deliver effective feedback, you need to know what it looks like. Here are some characteristics of effective feedback.

Effective feedback is timely. The closer in time you can deliver feedback to the performance, the more likely it is to be effective. The longer you delay your feedback, the less likely it is to be effective.

Effective feedback is specific. It should be about one observable thing. Words like "never" and "always" are signals that your feedback is not specific.

Effective feedback addresses only things you can observe. You can't directly observe attitude or motivation, so don't talk about those things. Instead, talk about what your team member said or did, or about the specifics of measurable performance.

Effective feedback is respectful. The person you're talking to did something that could have been done better. We all do that. Your objective is to improve performance, not "fix" a person.

Effective feedback is a conversation, not a lecture. If all you do is tell someone how to change, you may get compliance, but you're not likely to get buy-in. When you have a conversation about solving a performance problem, you involve your teammate in solving the problem.

Effective feedback ends with an agreement. Without agreement, your feedback session is just a chat. Before you wind up the session, you and your teammate should agree on what will change, how it will change, when it will change, and how you will evaluate the changed performance.

Now you know what effective feedback looks like. Let's shift to thinking about what you can do to deliver it.

You can use 4DCulture™ as a guide when you begin a conversation with a teammate about performance. Consider your relative positions on the different culture scales. That will help you anticipate difficult areas.

*Adapt your behavior so that it works best
with the person or situation you're facing.*

American managers deal with feedback in a unique way. In general, we don't have a problem with positive feedback. We love giving praise and telling people they're doing a good job. Negative feedback is a different story.

As I noted in the chapter on communication styles, USers are more indirect with negative feedback. Sometimes we mix in positive comments to soften the blow. According to the research, when we do that, a team member may hear only the positive. The negative may not come across clearly enough to some cultures or personalities.

Another common American tactic is to try to soften negative feedback with what scientists call "downgraders." They're phrases like "sort of" or "a little" or "kind of." That can be a good choice if the person you're speaking with has an Indirect Communication style. It won't be as effective with someone who is used to direct negative feedback, or perhaps when the manager is not speaking the employee's native language.

As you prepare for a feedback session, you might want to practice your initial description of the performance you want to change. Remember that it should be specific, observable, and respectful. During the session, you can use OAR™ to enhance the feedback process.

Using OAR™ for Feedback

Start by reviewing what they did and why it's important. Stick with the facts. You should be able to do this in a couple of sentences.

Observe their initial reaction. Be watchful for defensiveness or an emotional shutdown so that you can deal with it in the moment.

Ask them for their reaction to what you said. Then, wait for your teammate to talk. If you're a US manager, this can be tough, but wait, even if you're uncomfortable. Waiting until the other person speaks increases the possibility that you will have a real conversation. Sometimes you'll be surprised. You may discover that you didn't understand the situation correctly.

The goal is to have a conversation about improving performance and finish with an agreement about what will change, when it will change, and how you will measure the change. You should talk about any consequences, too.

After the session, part of your job as a manager is to follow up and make sure that agreement turns into a change in performance or behavior. Sometimes a single feedback session will result in the change you desire. Sometimes it will take more than one session.

Be aware that behavior can and should change immediately. Performance or learned skills may take a little longer to improve. As a manager, don't waste too much time on a situation in which behavior isn't changing quickly.

A Culture of Feedback

Individual feedback sessions with individual team members will certainly improve their performance and the team's performance, but a culture of feedback can have a huge impact on performance and morale and make your job much easier. You have a culture of feedback when all team members can and do offer effective feedback to each other. That includes you.

If you want to make this happen, you must teach the basic method for feedback that we've outlined in this chapter. You also must be willing to take feedback from team members. That may be particularly difficult for you if you grew up in a culture that values High Formality on the Formality scale, or you believe that the manager should always be the one giving feedback.

For many new managers, this is one of those areas where they must learn to be comfortable being uncomfortable. Accepting feedback gratefully from your direct reports is the most powerful thing you can do to create trust, credibility, and a positive team environment. A culture of feedback on your team is one of the best ways to improve performance and morale and make your job as a manager much easier, so it's worth the effort and the struggle.

Delivering effective feedback is a vital skill that you must master to be a great manager. It's only one kind of routine conversation with teammates, though. The other one is coaching.

COACHING

Organizations use several different models for coaching, but many of them can trace their roots back to Sir John Whitmore and his GROW model.

Whitmore was a famous and successful race car driver. When his driving career was over, he started a company to help people improve their performance. He developed his coaching model based on two observations: 1) People were more likely to own a solution or a decision that they had developed themselves. 2) Most people already had the knowledge to help develop the insights and solutions that were important to them.

The letters in Whitmore's GROW model stand for:

Goal: What do you want?
Reality: What's the situation now?
Options: What are the possible solutions?
Way Forward: What will you commit to?

Each of the letters stands for a question. That's what makes the GROW model a perfect companion to OAR™. Here's how we use OAR™ in a coaching situation.

Observe your teammate's body language and general mood. Observe if they appear uncomfortable or puzzled. As you observe, resist the urge to jump in and provide an answer.

Ask Questions. Ask the questions from the GROW model. Ask "What do you think?" and "How do you feel?"

and "What do you think will happen?" and "What do you think you should do?" These questions will allow your direct report to come up with his or her own answers.

React with suggestions, or by reflecting back what your teammate has said, or examples of possibilities, but allow them to struggle a little to find the answer that's right for them.

When you're planning a coaching session, remember that people who were raised in High Formality cultures may not be comfortable with being asked what they think they should do. They expect their boss or another authority figure to direct them. I encountered this when I was coaching some managers from India.

I began my sessions by saying that the purpose of the coaching session was to help them solve any issues or help them think about a goal to work toward. Then I asked a question about how things were going, but all the managers would say is that they really didn't have any issues and that things were fine. I tried asking my questions in different ways, but nothing seemed to work. I was stumped.

Then, one of the managers told me that he was glad I was there because he needed some mentoring. I didn't expect that, so I asked what he meant by "mentoring." The manager described a process that I would call "coaching." When I started my next coaching session, I tried calling it a "mentoring" session.

That just completely opened up the conversations. For those managers, being "mentored" meant that could share their thoughts and ideas. When some of your team members are at the high end of the Formality dimensions, you may have to train them so they understand that they will be asked for their ideas about what to do and that the coaching process will help them grow and develop.

What I just described is the way coaching might work in a longer coaching session—maybe thirty minutes to an hour in a one-on-one, for example. You have other opportunities to coach that aren't quite as formal. I like to think of them as spot coaching. Here's how it works:

A teammate approaches you with a problem or an opportunity. He or she describes the situation and asks you what they should do. You could just answer the question, but that would pass up an opportunity for coaching that will help your team member grow. So, instead of offering an answer, ask them, "What do you think you should do?" That can lead to a coaching conversation in which they develop both knowledge about what they should do and confidence that will help them be more independent and accountable in the future.

Coaching is a necessary skill that managers can use to empower their direct reports, delegate tasks, and scale themselves in order to grow their team or take on other projects.

PRESENTATIONS

Coaching and feedback are strictly one-on-one events. It's you and one other person, and you have the objective of helping them improve their performance or develop their skills and confidence. Presentations are different. When you make a presentation, you're out there in full view of everybody. That offers you some great opportunities.

When you're the presenter, you're a person of influence. When you're the presenter, you have an opportunity to demonstrate your knowledge and skills. When you're in front of a crowd, you stand out from the crowd. You might think that those benefits would result in everyone competing to be the one to present, but that doesn't happen.

Research tells us that speaking in front of others is really scary for a lot of people. There's an official term for it: "glossophobia," and some writers claim that people are more afraid of speaking in public than they are of death. I don't know about that, but I know that an awful lot of people are uncomfortable speaking in front of others and that many good managers avoid making presentations that could boost their career. Is that you?

If speaking to groups makes you uncomfortable, the best thing you can do is spend some time learning and developing your public-speaking skills. Training and preparation drive out fear and enable you to seize the opportunities that giving presentations offers you.

Most of the presentations you will make as a manager will fall into one of two groups: 1) Sharing the results of some work that you and your team have done. 2) Making a presentation to persuade others to support your ideas. Either way, you should do some planning based on the Thought Patterns of the people who will be in your audience.

Thought Patterns should give you a clue about the order of presentation. Since you're a US manager, you're likely to be surrounded by other people who grew up in US business culture. Most of those people are action-oriented. They want to know your conclusions first; after that, you can share the process you used to reach your conclusions or recommendations.

For process-oriented people, the preference is reversed. They don't want to know your conclusion or recommendation until they know what research and reasoning you used to get there.

For example, I worked with a sales team in the US who had gotten strict instructions from Europe to use their newly global "standardized" sales presentation in every location with every client. They were highly successful in Europe, so it was tried and tested. However, when the US received it, they realized they couldn't show the first sixteen slides to US customers or they would lose them. Those slides contained the history of the company, the training the engineers get, and awards the company has won in Europe. Nothing that would be familiar to, or interest, the US customer. Slide 17 started with the product line and what the company can do for its customers.

Now, it gets interesting when you have a mixed group. I recommend starting with the vision or results, sharing how you got there—high-level—and then come in again with your results and ask at the end. But leave plenty of room for those who are process-oriented and need more details upfront to ask questions, discuss, or push back on what you've shared.

Presenting is key in establishing credibility and visibility for yourself and promoting your team's work. Get good at it, and you'll make a fine career.

MEETINGS

"Meetings are a waste of time!"

"Why do we have so many meetings?"

"How can I get my work done if I have to spend all my time in meetings?"

We complain a lot about meetings, but some meetings give all meetings a bad rap. Some meetings shouldn't be called at all. They are a complete waste of time and a drain on productivity. Other meetings are inefficient and boring. They suck up time that team members could use to do something productive.

That's true, but meetings are also an important way that effective teams get their work done. You should have a meeting anytime that you need to get people together at the same time to make progress. That's usually not simple reporting. Most reporting can be handled much better with e-mail, project-management software, or intranet postings. There are two times when it makes sense to get people together, either in the same room or via technology, at the same time:

1. Regularly scheduled meetings set the cadence for work. Some teams hold a regular daily or weekly check-in meeting. In those meetings, people usually say a little bit about what they're working on and what kind of help they need from the rest of the team. Regular check-in meetings usually include a short self-report by each team member to help build relationships and understanding, too. Check-in meetings should be held at the same time every day or week. They should follow the same general format every time.

2. Other meetings are called to deal with a single issue. Whether you're having a problem on a project or difficulties with a customer, a meeting can help you sort things out.

Those meetings should deal with only a single issue. The only people who should attend the meeting are those necessary to make progress on the issue. Those people who need only to be kept informed can be brought up to date with an e-mail, audio, or video report.

As a manager, you're responsible for the performance of your group. That means that, most of the time, you will be the one calling a meeting. You can help team members develop by giving them the freedom to call a meeting and training them to do it well.

I've witnessed many managers, especially new managers, who think their job in a meeting is to be in charge. You won't get many of the benefits of effective meetings that way, though. Instead, if you want to get good at doing meetings, become a great facilitator. This is where your OAR™ skills come in really handy.

When you don't have to "run" the meeting, you can spend more time observing what happens. Pay attention to body language. Watch for puzzled or angry facial expressions. Listen to tones of voice and word choice.

Analyze what you hear. Ask questions. Then do something (React), and watch for what happens.

You'll be a better facilitator if you've taken the time to learn about the people on your team. 4DCulture™ will help you identify and prepare for problems that have cultural roots. You'll also learn about your team members through routine conversations and careful observation.

Facilitating a meeting is one of the most challenging parts of your job as a manager. Issues, personalities, and business challenges are all in play all at the same time. They're also a critical part of managing a team, which we'll cover in the next chapter.

CHAPTER 13

MANAGING TEAMS

Managing teams has to be one of the hardest parts of a manager's job. Getting a team up and running, motivated, engaged, and performing at a high level takes hard work, time, and lots of attention. It's hard even if you're on familiar ground with team members from your own culture, age group, or gender. It's even harder if there are cross-cultural issues.

Remember the story of the French manager with the team in Mexico? That manager had a hard time figuring out what was going on. Then there was the manager from Japan managing his team of engineers in the US. That didn't start out well.

When you're new to the team or you inherit a team, that adds challenges. And, since no team stays the same forever, there are the challenges created when team members leave or the team adds new ones.

In this chapter, I'll describe a model I use in my workshops that helps managers all over the world manage teams more effectively. I'll offer some tips and tricks as well as how to manage virtual teams successfully.

Let me start with a situation that may be familiar to you.

A local team in the US at a tech start-up was running well. Everyone was really excited about the new project they were working on. People were replying-all to every e-mail, cheering each other on, there were lots of "please" and "thank yous"—good energy all around. It was a high-visibility project, the new shiny thing with company executives. New people were getting hired into the team. The team lead was communicating heavily with everyone.

Then, gradually, as the project kickoff ended and the go-live was running smoothly, the executive excitement waned, the team lead got distracted with other projects, and the energy quieted. There was one interteam conflict, new members were feeling neglected, and there was a restructuring of leadership in the department. Everything changed in a matter of months.

THE TUCKMAN MODEL

This isn't uncommon for teams and projects. In fact, I would go so far as to say it's normal. Luckily, there's a way to manage it better. I recommend using a model developed by Dr. Bruce Tuckman in 1965. It's called the Tuckman Model, and it's still in use because it works for teams around the world. It has four stages: Forming, Storming, Norming, and Performing.

Forming

Forming happens when the team is coming together for the first time or when a new member or members join the team. Forming also happens when a new manager takes over. The atmosphere is polite, and people are cautious, feeling each other out.

In this stage, it's important to emphasize processes, clarify roles, and direct or train team members so they understand what's expected of them and how to meet deliverables.

Storming

Storming happens when the team starts to push back, debate, even have conflicts. You might hear things like, "Well, at my previous company, we did it this way." Team members start to vie for power.

In this stage, it's really important to surface disagreement and mediate conflicts. Using OAR™ will help you understand what's truly behind the storm.

Norming

After a while, the storm passes, and it's quiet again This stage is about reforming or "norming." As the manager, you can reset rules and procedures, restate roles, and ensure that the overall mission of the team is clear. Team members should be moving from a state of "What's in it for me?" to seeing themselves as part of a solid team.

Performing

The atmosphere in this stage is one of high energy and comfort. The team is functioning at a high level, they are finishing each other's sentences, passing the baton easily and quickly.

Your job as a manager is to get out of the way but still remain available to the team. Support, cheerleading, and advocacy are what it's all about.

CROSS-CULTURAL TEAMS

4DCulture™ is an important model to master when managing local or global teams. You'll need to understand the individual needs and interests of your team members. In addition to the typical incentives like money, promotions, or recognition, you'll want to understand how cultural aspects like family obligations, commitment to friendships, or the government's role in society influence team member behavior. All of these impact the relationship to the company, manager, team, and customers.

VIRTUAL TEAMS

Here are three interesting statistics I'd like to share with you specific to managing virtual teams:

1. If a team meets even once face-to-face during the course of a project, it will increase productivity by 50 percent.
2. To mimic spontaneous interaction of face-to-face teams, virtual teams need to intentionally connect three times more per week than a brief status update, even if it's only to chit-chat for fifteen minutes.
3. The statistics show face-to-face is ten times more effective than phone calls, and the phone is ten times more effective than e-mail. E-mail is still the default team communication tool in most companies. We need to consider picking up the phone or connecting over a video source more often.

Additionally, there are three very important ways to look at managing teams successfully. They're particularly relevant in virtual teams:

Creating Context
Creating Community
Cosharing Leadership

When teams understand the context or what, why, and who, they are more apt to buy into the overall mission and the individual deliverables they are responsible for.

A sense of community within the team and greater organization is also shown to increase engagement and productivity. When working virtually, it's particularly hard to feel a part of something. Going into the local office one day a week to network and meet with colleagues is one way to increase a feeling of community.

Another way is to set up home offices with company or team "swag," reminding the individual team member what they are a part of, what the team stands for, etc.

As a manager, sharing leadership responsibility is one of the best strategies to involve team members. Each individual should be empowered to take the lead in a team meeting, take charge of a piece of a project or a whole project, as well as be accountable for specific results in their area of expertise. In a leadership role, team members will feel more responsible for outcomes and more connected to the team and project.

Of course, you'll want to consider the 4DCulture™ model and, in particular, the dimension of Formality. Setting expectations will help individuals understand, accept, and appreciate their leadership role.

Managing teams is challenging and rewarding. Please see the appendices for several quotes by experienced managers on how and why they enjoy their manager role as it pertains to working with their teams.

NEXT STEPS AS A NEW GLOBAL MANAGER

What's Next?

In this book, I've tried to give you the tools to become a New Global Manager. I don't know exactly what's next for you, but I do know that it will have three characteristics:

1. **You'll be part of something big.** The United States is a gigantic place. It's the third-largest country in the world, whether you're measuring by population or land area. And you'll be working as a manager in the world's largest economy, according to the World Bank. So, you'll have a wide array of opportunities to apply what you learned here.

2. **You'll do important work.** Managers are the glue that holds organizations together. As a manager, you're the one most responsible for the morale and the productivity of your team. You have the opportunity to make a difference in your company and in the lives of your team members.

3. **You'll be working in a time filled with challenges and opportunity.** We're living in times of great change, in both technology and society. The United States has the most diverse population in the world. Business is more global than it's ever been, with more companies from other countries doing business here, and with US-based corporations doing more and more of their business in other countries.

The way we do our work is changing, too. Technology has made it possible to do business twenty-four hours a day and seven days a week. The combination of technology and increasingly global business means that the teams that you work with will include people who do most of their work somewhere other than where you are.

I believe that calls for a new kind of manager, the kind I call a New Global Manager. You'll have to do the same kind of things that managers have always done and that company training and books cover in great detail. But you also must do something more, and that's what this book is about.

You'll work in the new world of global business. A lot will be the same as it's always been, but a lot will be different. I've shared information and developed some rules that will help you thrive in this new and exciting environment.

The following is a summary of Melissa's Management Rules and other key learnings in the book:

ADAPT YOUR BEHAVIOR SO THAT IT WORKS BEST WITH THE PERSON OR SITUATION YOU'RE FACING.

The most effective managers have always been the ones who modified their behavior to fit the situation. Business situations increasingly include more and more people with different personal, cultural, and organizational understandings. You'll be more likely to succeed if you adapt to a behavior rather than expect people to adapt to you.

YOU WON'T COME UP WITH THE RIGHT BEHAVIOR OR DECISION JUST BY THINKING ABOUT IT. YOU NEED TO DO SOMETHING, SEE IF IT WORKS, AND MODIFY, IF NECESSARY.

It would be nice if I could give you a recipe for every management situation that you'll face. Then you'd know exactly what to do. That's impossible. You'll be more effective if you do some homework and then try out for yourself.

Some of the time, it will work right away, and some of the time, it won't. If it doesn't, you need to use the OAR™ tool. You Observe what's happening. You Ask Questions to help you decide what to do next. And then you React by changing your behavior. Once you've done that, the cycle starts again. Observe—Ask Questions—React.

YOU MAKE CHOICES AND DECISIONS BASED ON YOUR CULTURE, BUT OTHER PEOPLE MAKE DECISIONS BASED ON THEIR CULTURE.

Your initial actions make perfect sense to you. But they may not make sense to the person you've encountered. They will filter their understanding through their own cultural and experiential lens. 4DCulture™ will help you figure out what's going on. Then you need to be quick on your feet, so you can adapt quickly and effectively.

OAR™ IS YOUR TOOL OF CHOICE TO DEAL WITH CULTURAL ISSUES AND THE SURPRISES A FAST-CHANGING BUSINESS ENVIRONMENT WILL SPRING ON YOU.

Sometimes you'll want to jump right in and do something, but you're more likely to get a good outcome if you take the time to observe and ask questions before you react.

At other times, you'll be tempted to stay with your original plan or idea, even if it doesn't seem to be working. At those times, you need to Observe, Ask Questions, and then React with something different.

YOU MUST GET USED TO BEING COMFORTABLE WITH BEING UNCOMFORTABLE.

As you move through your days and your career, you will encounter many situations that are new and puzzling. They're likely to make you uncomfortable. That's okay. Take being uncomfortable as a challenge to find the best thing to do.

EVERY PERSON IS DIFFERENT. USE CULTURAL TENDENCIES AS A STARTING POINT, BUT TREAT THEM AS GUIDELINES, NOT RULES.

The 4DCulture™ tool gives you a way to analyze the cultural forces that are in play in any situation. I don't know how many cultural forces there are altogether, but it's a lot. I chose four cultural dimensions that, based on my experience, are most likely to influence your encounters in the workplace. The four dimensions are: Thought Patterns, Time, Communication Style, and Formality Level.

NO ONE IS THE SAME AS YOU. YOU'LL CONSTANTLY BE SURPRISED BY THE WAY PEOPLE BEHAVE, SO YOU WILL ALWAYS BE IN LEARNING SITUATIONS.

It's a fast-changing world, and you'll never be done learning. Stay curious. Investigate and ask questions. Take notes on what surprises you and what you did and how things worked. Make notes about how to do things differently next time. The best managers keep asking and learning for their entire life.

This is the end of the book, but it's the beginning of your exciting management journey. Practice using the 4DCulture™ tool to analyze situations and shorten your learning curve. Use the OAR™ tool habitually to modify your behavior so you're more likely to be successful.

I don't know what's ahead for you, except that you will face challenges that are fun, interesting, difficult—and different from the ones you face today. I hope you use what you learn here to meet those challenges more effectively.

WISDOM FROM THE TRENCHES

The following tips are in the form of quotes from experienced managers whom I interviewed for the book. I wanted some examples, tips, and tricks from the trenches. The full list of interview participants is in the front of the book under "Thank You."

The first category here references the cultural dimensions in 4DCulture™.

Thought Patterns

" . . . when you're working globally, the process is just as important as the solution."

Formality

" . . . I'll let you know what I know and what I don't know and I'm not going to be—don't come to me and just look for orders."

The next grouping of quotes references management skills.

Coaching

"Before you try to anticipate what someone is going to ask you about, just *Listen* and take a moment to pause and really hear what someone is telling you. Ask lots of questions."

Managing Teams

"But when you come across high-potential talent, two things occur. One, they challenge you a lot back. But, more importantly, they can take on more and more and more tasks, and then it becomes a challenge on just how to manage them. But you almost feel kind of like you're chasing the ball a little bit trying to keep them challenged. And it's a fun experience. It really challenges how you lead."

"You just have to constantly be on top of your priorities—like, "Hey, I know we talked about a million different things in a day. Let's be clear. The top three priorities are A, B, and C. And you just have to keep putting that message down to the right levels and organization. Because otherwise people just get tied up in the day-to-day, and they lose sight of it."

Presentations and Sales

" . . . when one of our best Product Managers came to Pittsburgh, he was tasked with presenting the results of a market study, investigating the issues of a product in the mining market. The original plan was to present for two hours. He was presenting to mostly US colleagues, and for the first thirty minutes, he was just talking about the approach. So instead of sharing the results, he was saying, 'Yeah, and then I analyzed this and that, and I used such and such a tool,' etc. You know what happened—right? He drove the people nuts. They were basically shaking their heads— 'What the heck? He has just sixty minutes, and he's talking about the fricking approach for thirty minutes.'

"So what it comes back to is: Don't apply your own rules. And that's true, of course, not just for management rules but in general. So whatever works in your own culture doesn't necessarily work in other people's culture, and you can extract a lot. And in this case people looked at him as an academic, as someone who was not really goal oriented, someone who was missing the boat.

"And, of course, in reality, he was exactly the opposite. He was one of the most intelligent and most results-oriented people we've had in product management. But that's not the impression he left. So, prepare your folks, your people, prepare yourself, at least with regard to the most important aspects of different cultures. And try to adjust your style to it every once in a while."

Feedback and Coaching

"I was at another company, and I had a pretty senior person reporting to me. And you know, 90 percent of the time, she performed extremely well. And we had a very— I'll call it a *really high-risk*—situation. We were working on a project that had some pretty significant people and the potential for legal impact. She made a mistake that I thought could have been a disaster. It wasn't. but it could have been a disaster, so I immediately shifted to coaching her about it, and I probably coached her too strongly. And I started really monitoring what she was doing and checking in with her a lot. And that made her feel like she was being monitored too much, or watched too much. And so she clammed up and really didn't take the initiative that I wanted her to take. And when I thought about that and analyzed it, I realized that I had overreacted. Everybody makes mistakes. I should have just had a quick coaching session with her, and said, 'You know, I trust you. If you have any other questions, feel free to come to me. Let's just let this slide and keep doing what you're doing.' That's the approach I should have taken with her."

Managing High-Performance Teams

"I've been challenged on that by a couple of employees in the past who said, 'Well, we would like to have helped with that.' We recently used a consultant from an outside consulting firm to come in and help us find solutions on a particular project. I thought I was very clever for bringing in outside help. It was a little expensive, but we knew we were going to get this solved. We were quite deep into before it started to filter back to me that quite a few people were really disappointed that we looked to the outside for somebody to take this bull by the horns and run with it. It was a bit of a shock to me. I thought this was a good use of our funding—to bring in outside help. The feedback was, 'We've been looking for opportunities to express ourselves and show you that we're more than just transaction-analysis-based people. An opportunity came up, and you got somebody from the outside to do it.'"

"I think you have to be sensitive to global differences to begin with and not always make it about our own time zone. It's better to do a face-to-face with the person at some point in time, because that's the way you learn about the person. It helps you to kind of understand their style and the culture and nuances."

"From my perspective the two most important aspects about management are 1) setting the right direction which actually is setting the targets, the action plan. Call it 'strategy,' call it a 'probe'—whatever, but you need to understand where you are heading. And 2) a transparent and easily understood method of bringing it across to every employee in the company. But you cannot assume that people understand where you are heading the first time you tell them. They need to hear it again and again and again."

"I tell my people that I'm extremely well paid to work all hours, weekends, what have you. But should you receive an e-mail from me late at night or on the weekend, I do not expect you to respond. This is your free time. Ignore me. It's just that I'm working through my inbox—this is 'expectation management.' I'm quite happy for you to wait to pick up that e-mail Monday morning when you come into the office. If there's something urgent, I know how to get ahold of you. You can rely on me to be there when there's trouble."

"I think with virtual teams, picking up the phone is vital. Talk to the people on a regular basis, as a team and as individuals. Use webcams, so that people see each other. It's simple, but we all these days have laptops with webcams. I sometimes say, 'I don't want to switch the webcam on. I'm having a bad hair day.' People laugh, but I switch it on anyway. It's very much an effort to bring people together. And we all know that we face budget constraints, so personal meetings of big teams are very hard to organize simply for budget reasons. So you really have to make an effort to bring these people together even if it's only for a video conference. Use that platform to speak."

"Sometimes I think the more you learn about individuals, the more it is not about cultural sensitivity but more specific to the individual. If today I've got a conversation with someone from Japan, and tomorrow I've got a conversation with someone from Italy, those will likely be very, very different conversations."

"Yes, you can read books to gain cultural sensitivity, but anecdotes that others tell you and your own experiences in the country may be the most helpful to learn that sensitivity."

These nuggets of wisdom help define and discuss the role of a manager.

MANAGER'S ROLE

"I'm far more interested in people than in numbers—whether the share price went up by 2 percent or whether our revenues went up by 5 percent. I'm far more interested in individuals. I think I retain that kind of interest in the group and developing individuals from my days as a school teacher. The journey of an individual and watching them grow is way more important to me than knowing if we collected an extra $10,000 this month. We have metrics to measure how we deliver results, but my happier moments are when I see people able to progress and develop. We should be about transforming people, growing people, hiring internally, giving people opportunities both inside and outside the room."

"A good manager, I think, adapts to different situations. If you need to be an extrovert and fire people up and motivate people, then you do that. But if you need to take a step back and be much more of a listener, you should do that, too. I don't know if I'm always successful in doing it, but I love it, because for me it's putting fire within people, instead of under people. I strongly believe that people don't follow title—at least I don't—but people follow people. That's what it's all about for me—delivering fantastic results through people."

"Recognizing what people are great at and taking risks on people is really important. Give them an opportunity to shine."

"We've got to stay inquisitive to understand what makes people tick because we are all so different. We can guess, but that gets you only so far. I think asking helps you understand and it really helps to establish trust with your direct reports. It shows that you care. It shows that you are really trying to set them up for success.

"Building that into every one-on-one meeting. Ask, 'How is this going? What about your job has excited you the most in the last week?' I think constantly checking in on that really helps your people grow."

"I once had a manager who took the time to not only describe a future that I could visualize, but who actually brought me in to multiple scenarios where I could watch her do the exact work that I would be doing. The second thing about that manager is that she would never let me just do the job that was required in the job description. She would always say, 'Here are the things that I'll model for you, expose you to, and then, you're going to do them.' I think that changed not only my career trajectory but also how I actually lead today because I try to create those same experiences for people."

"A good manager not only advocates a position but also draws out people's ideas and their feelings. It's important to be really clear on what the expectations are. But let them develop the 'how' in terms of how they're going to get the task or the responsibility accomplished. There may be more than one path to a great solution. Review the progress as you move forward."

"A good manager will let people experiment—even if they fail. Because nobody gets it perfect the first time. So people have to make mistakes, and learn from those mistakes, and grow and do it better and better over time."

These quotes generally share tips and tricks about communicating effectively as a manager.

COMMUNICATION

"Very clear and effective communication—as well as clear and effective follow-up—are paramount. A lot of managers will make the comment, 'I shouldn't have to follow-up on this or that,' but I think the reality is that you do have to. You have to communicate what you expect from the individuals you are working with. You have to follow up and continue to reiterate these messages."

"You have to stay ahead of the curve and not become complacent. Often, once we put our team in place, we have a tendency to kind of sit back—especially if we consider the people we've chosen to be very capable. Stay ahead of the curve, whether it be technology or your industry or certain trends in the marketplace. And use those tools and what you've learned to continually challenge your team."

"I would ask somebody who wants to become a manager, 'Are you sure you really want it?' Are you prepared to go the whole way, meaning are you prepared to spend a large part of your time with people management?'"

"I had a manager once, and, in retrospect, what was super inspiring was understanding what he was really going through. On the inside, he was bleeding, and he was terrified. But on the outside, he communicated an unwavering confidence in the ability of the team to do great things and for the company to become great."

"It's hard to be a good leader. It's easy to succumb to your own fears, your own biases, and your own concerns and not think about the big picture and inspire and push. I think it takes a certain personality. It takes being aware, and it takes maturity."

"It's really important for a manager to recognize that their job is to 'clear the brush,' meaning being out ahead of your team, kind of cutting through, cutting the path, so that they can move swiftly forward on whatever it is that you've asked them to do."

"It is my responsibility to advocate for my team and advocate for the higher purpose of my team and what it can bring to the larger organization. I must convince people what resources are needed, and then my responsibility is to persuade people to listen to the input of my team."